MW01255167

Yes I Con

United Fakes of America

Lloyd Billingsley

A Centershot Book

The persons and events in this book are factual. Any resemblance to fictional characters and imaginary events is entirely coincidental.

ISBN 978-0-9968581-7-5

First edition 2020

Printed in the United States of America

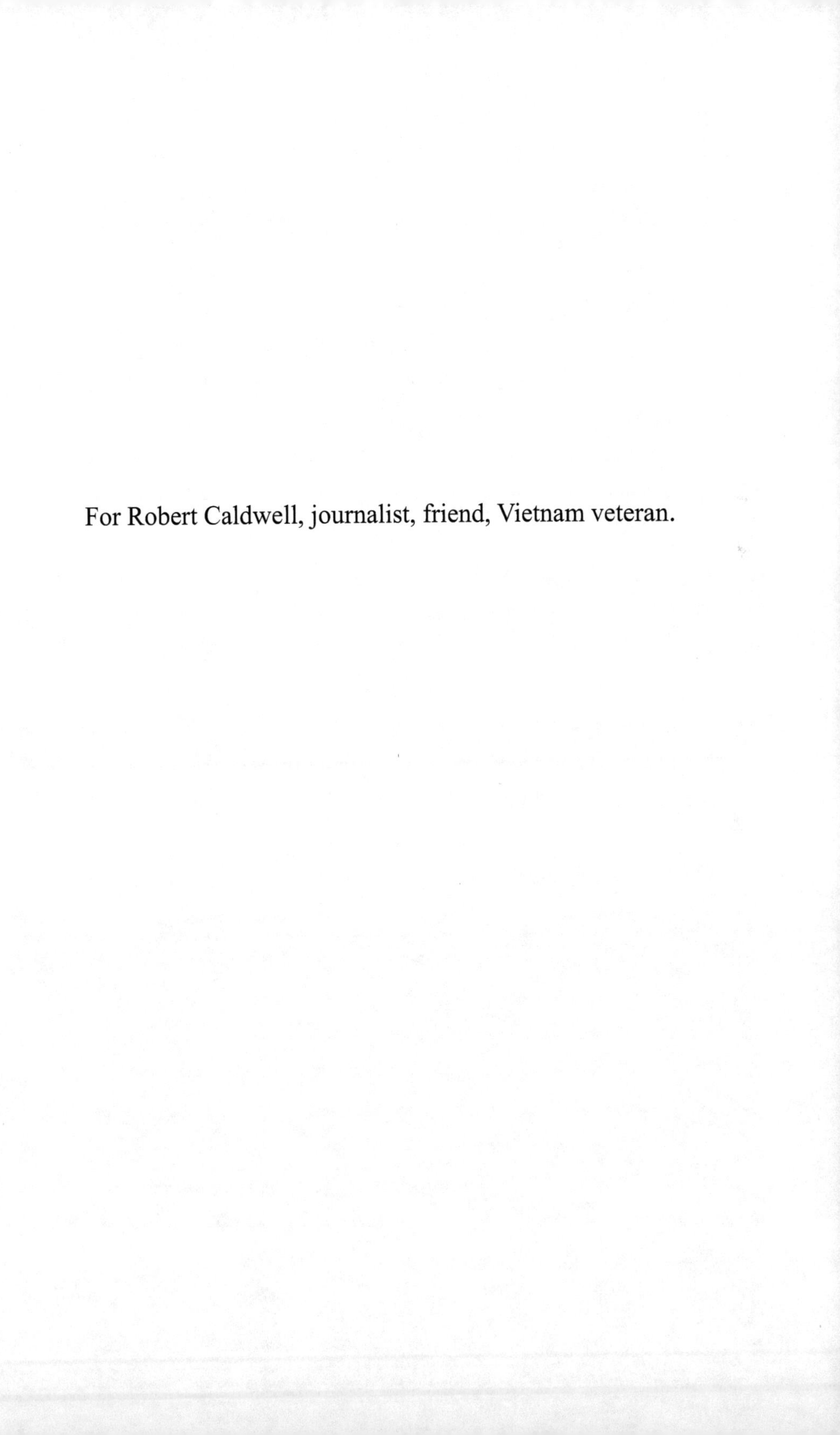

For Robert Caldwell, journalist, friend, Vietnam veteran.

From enthusiasm to imposture the step is perilous and slippery. The conscience may slumber in a mixed and middle state between self-illusion and voluntary fraud.

—Edward Gibbon,
Decline and Fall of the Roman Empire, Vol. 5

Table of Contents

Foreword: The Syndrome Beyond Satire

In October of 2019, Democrats held a presidential debate in Ohio, hosted by the Cable News Network. One of the 12 presidential hopefuls was Hawaii Rep. Tulsi Gabbard, 38, a decorated veteran who joined the U.S. military after the terrorist attacks of September 11, 2001. Right up front, CNN's Anderson Cooper asked the candidates if they favored the impeachment of president Donald Trump. Most of the Democrats came out strong for impeachment, as the studio audience cheered. Tulsi Gabbard said the inquiry should go forward, but as she also recalled, "Donald Trump won the election in 2016." The stunned silence that followed was predictable, and full of significance.

In full view of the nation, Tulsi Gabbard acknowledged that Hillary Clinton *lost* the 2016 election, a clear violation of the Democrat speech code and leftist eschatology. People of the left, who call themselves "progressives," believe history is on their side, so if the progressive candidate loses it must be due to trickery by the opponent. True to form, the former First Lady and Secretary of State did not acknowledge that she lost the 2016 election to Donald Trump, and lately she had been telling anybody who would listen, "obviously, I can beat him again." So as the former First Lady imagined, she was running for reelection.

Days after the debate, Hillary Clinton accused fellow Democrat Tulsi Gabbard of being a "Russian asset," already supported by Russian websites, bots and such. POTUS 44's UN boss Samantha Power tweeted that Gabbard would be would be "a huge windfall for Trump, Assad, Putin, Xi." How clever Vladimir Putin had been, Greg Gutfeld quipped on Fox News, to task Tulsi Gabbard to enlist in the U.S. military, run for Congress in Hawaii, and now seek the White

House on an anti-war platform. That brought some laughs, but the events were already beyond satire.

In the ongoing impeachment inquiry, intelligence committee boss Adam Schiff performed Donald Trump as a Sollozzo character from *The Godfather*, telling the president of Ukraine that if he wanted his money, the Trump crime family needed something in return. As the transcript of the actual call revealed, Trump made no such demand. The vaunted "whistleblower," more accurately a conspirator, is a partisan Democrat who worked with Joe Biden and reported hearsay about a conversation by the president anybody could read. And as it turned out, the inspector general who took the complaint seriously had been a player in the previous high-concept drama, in which Donald Trump colludes with Putin to steal the election from Hillary Clinton.

As the ad copy had it, Putin loves Trump and hates Hillary. The United States Department of Justice appointed former FBI boss Robert Mueller to look into it. He hired a squad of partisan Democrat *sturmtruppen*, and after more than two years of searching high and low, they found no collusion. On the other hand, some of the dialog did prove revealing.

FBI counterintelligence boss Peter Strzok headed up "Midyear Exam," an operation to clear Hillary Clinton from any criminal charges for destroying evidence, so she could remain in the 2016 presidential race. Strzok and his FBI girlfriend Lisa Page were convinced that Hillary was a lock, but just in case, they had an insurance policy, another intelligence operation known as "Crossfire Hurricane." That blew up a destructive storm but uncovered no collusion between Trump and Russia. Amidst the wreckage, a different sort of collusion emerged.

"POTUS wants to know everything we're doing," Page texted Strzok. For all but the willfully blind, POTUS 44, formerly known as Barry Soetoro, approved and closely monitored the operation. From the start he had been transforming the United States from a democracy into an authoritarian state whose outgoing president picks his successor and rigs the system in her favor. He had eight years to leverage the Deep State drones in his favor, but the operation failed and all hell broke loose.

Trump Derangement Syndrome, a widespread and bipartisan affliction, surged to dizzying heights of rage and plunged to fathomless depths of absurdity. On reflection, the syndrome wasn't about POTUS 44, POTUS 45, the wife of POTUS 42, or the corruption of the Deep State and its media allies, as interesting as all that may be.

The syndrome beyond satire is a deep-seated detachment from truth, facts, and objective reality altogether, the dictatorship of the subjunctive mood. This dynamic had been on display with POTUS 32, surged mightily with POTUS 44, and at this writing continues unabated.

Lloyd Billingsley, somewhere in North America, December, 2019.

Presideception and Consequences

In July of 2018, the Franklin D. Roosevelt Presidential Library and Museum in Hyde Park, New York, revealed a seven-second stretch of black-and-white 16mm film shot by New York tourist Fred Hill on April 22, 1935, during the White House Easter Egg Roll.

"As Hill filmed," explained Michael Ruane of the *Washington Post*, "President Franklin D. Roosevelt, who had been disabled by polio 14 years before, emerged and — with the help of a cane and his body-guard — walked unsteadily to wave to the crowd."

By 2018, nearly 100 years since the event, few regarded the 32nd president of the United States as anything less than able bodied. The unveiling of the film gave them more reason to be puzzled.

Museum officials told Ruane that newsreel cameramen were warned against filming FDR while he was walking, "lest his disability be shown." The president could walk only with heavy leg braces and assistance, and only for short distances. Mr. Hill, whose grandson donated the footage, was unaware of the rules and just kept filming.

As Roosevelt biographer Goeffrey Ward explained, Roosevelt used a wheelchair, often had to be carried by aides, and sometimes crawled from one room to another on the floor. Even so, FDR had "this amazing ability to look as if absolutely nothing was wrong," when it was. He could also act like "the most carefree man in the world," which he wasn't.

"People didn't want him to be handicapped," Ward explained. "We were in the middle of a depression. They wanted their president to be a vigorous, able person, and he wanted to fulfill that role."

Franklin Delano Roosevelt was not a vigorous, able person and as Ruane notes, the president's "efforts to conceal the extent of his disability, are rich chapters in American history." Even so, the concealment was not revealed in detail until 1985, when Dodd, Mead and Company published Hugh Gregory Gallagher's *FDR's Splendid Deception: The moving story of Roosevelt's massive disability – and the intense efforts to conceal it from the public*. This book emerged a full 40 years, nearly half a century, after FDR's death in the waning days of World War II, and more than 60 years after the onset of polio that brought on the disability. Long before, Roosevelt was a national figure.

Born in 1882 in Hyde Park, New York and raised in luxury, Roosevelt served four years in the New York State Senate and during World War I became Assistant Secretary of the Navy. In 1920, FDR was the Democrat candidate for vice president under James Cox.

The next year, he suffered the attack of polio, and as Gallagher notes, he was "anxious that press should not know how severely paralyzed he had become." A whispering campaign contended he was unable to handle the duties of the presidency and *Time* magazine said FDR was mentally qualified but "utterly unfit physically."

FDR's close associate Louis Howe "constantly misled reporters" and worked out "a scheme to transfer Roosevelt without reporters discovering just how ill he really was." And as a public figure, reporters had good reason to report on him.

He ran again for national office in 1928 and 1930, when he campaigned in an open touring car. As Gallagher recalls, "FDR had made it a rule, during his first campaign for governor, that photographers were not to take pictures of him looking crippled or helpless." As during his entire career, they obeyed with startling fidelity. At the time of Gallagher's book, there were 35,000 still photos of FDR in his presidential library, but only two photos of him in a wheelchair. Not a single newsreel showed him being lifted, carried or pushed in his chair.

"No movies of me getting out of the machine, boys," FDR used to tell the cameramen. In similar style, not a single editorial cartoon showed him physically impaired, and many portrayed him as a running, jumping man of action. This was long before television and FDR knew how to play the part.

"He used his cigarette holder to suggest confidence and good cheer," Gallagher explains, "his old-fashioned pince-nez glasses reminded people of their schoolteachers and of Woodrow Wilson. They bespoke stability, responsibility. His old fedora campaign hat was as familiar as an old shoe; his naval cape expressed dignity and drama. The complete package of props, together with the characteristic tilt of the head, the wave of the hand, the laugh, the smile, made FDR seem to the American people as familiar, as close as a family member."

Gallagher, also stricken with polio, was a lifelong disability advocate and ardent admirer of FDR. But as he acknowledged, "Roosevelt also had some less attractive traits. He was a manipulative man, devious and, on occasion, even sadistic. While he was often thoughtful of others, he could also be quite ruthless."

On the devious side, "he was really quite deceptive in reply to direct questions. When a newspaper editor charged that Roosevelt was still wheelchair bound, FDR shot back, "As a matter of fact, I don't use a wheelchair at all except a little kitchen chair on wheels to get about my room while dressing . . . and solely for the purpose of saving time." It was, in effect, the big lie, and the press went along for the ride.

FDR's handlers insisted that he was never lifted in public and never seen in a wheelchair. In 1932, when a speaker's podium was not bolted down, FDR crashed to the floor. Reporters witnessed the fall but took no photos and the incident failed to turn up in their stories. Once in the White House, FDR imposed rules "which were always obeyed," as Gallagher notes. When reporters asked about the handicap, press secretary Steve Early told them "it's not a story," but it was.

FDR's handicap was less of a burden in the White House, and the president could deploy the vast resources of the federal government to maintain his deception. If the president and his aides spotted a photographer breaking the rules, they would point out the offender and the Secret Service would seize the camera and expose the film, like the mobster Barzini in *The Godfather*.

As Gallagher noted, the Secret Service "built ramps for his use at every point. These were not simply ramps for the president's chair; upon occasion, the Secret Service would actually raise the entire level of a street to the level of the building entrance by means of temporary but extensive wooden trestles and scaffolding." These extensive measures allowed the FDR to appear to "walk" from his car into a building without undue effort. Despite the massive efforts, things did not always go as planned.

At the 1936 Democrat convention, as FDR reached out his hand to poet Edwin Markham, a knee lock on his leg brace snapped. As Gallagher showed, the president's handlers were well prepared.

"As FDR went down, they closed in, forming a tight circle, blocking the President from view. To the unsuspecting in the crowd it appeared the President had been momentarily engulfed by the welcome he was receiving. Only a very few of the people on the platform were aware of what happened, and they did not talk about it. The pool of reporters were aware of the accident, but as usual did not report it. The entire nation listening to the live broadcast on the radio were told nothing. It was a nonevent."

In 1943, while visiting wounded soldiers, "Roosevelt allowed himself to be seen in but two ways; standing or seated in an open car." A special four-engine C54 called *The Sacred Cow* boasted a cabin designed for FDR and his wheelchair, complete with an elevator.

During the 1944 campaign in New York City, Roosevelt rode in an open car for more than four hours and was "seen by millions, looked cheerful, animated, conversing, waving, throwing his head back with that famous contagious laugh. . . . It seemed evident to all that day in New York that he was as strong, as resilient as ever."

The press and the public had no clue what was happening behind the scenes.

"At points along the parade route the Secret Service had commandeered garage space," Gallagher recalled. "As the presidential cavalcade passed the garage, the president's car was turned out of the parade into the warmth of the heated building. Secret Service agents quickly lifted the president from the car and stretched him out full length on blankets laid on the floor. They removed his clothes down to the skin. He was toweled dry and given a rubdown. He was redressed in dry clothes, brandy was poured down his throat, and he was lifted back into the car. The pit stop was quickly done and the president was soon back in the cavalcade."

As in 1936 and 1940, FDR won reelection, but after his inauguration speech on January 20, 1945, "he never stood on braces or walked again." Two days later, FDR departed for Yalta, where it would become clear that the president's disability was not merely physical. To reverse the older charge of *Time* magazine, the partially paralyzed president had become utterly unfit mentally.

For Gallagher, an admirer who approved of the president's deception, "the man who seemed so little crippled by his handicap was, in fact, severely emotionally crippled." And as his paralysis progressed, so did the inevitable mental incompetence.

As World War II played out FDR showed "a curious indecision" and "distinct difficulty in organizing his thoughts." He would stare into space, slack-jawed, and took no briefings. During 16 months of decline, "only a very few persons on his immediate staff were aware of how marked it had become," Gallagher explains. "And they were reluctant to admit, even to themselves, how serious it was."

After the 1939 Stalin-Hitler pact, Nazi Germany and the USSR both invaded Poland, and Stalin also attacked Finland. These actions prompted FDR publicly to condemn the Soviet Union as a "dictatorship as absolute as any other dictatorship in the world."

In October of 2019, Brett Baier of Fox News came out with *Three Days at the Brink: FDR's Daring Gamble to Win World War II.* According to Gallagher, FDR had no daring plan of any kind.

As his conditioned worsened, FDR outsourced more of his views to the pro-Stalin Harry Hopkins, whom Gallagher describes as "his trusted, ailing, wartime advisor." FDR fully approved of the 1943 film *Mission to Moscow*, blatant propaganda that justified Stalin's purges, the Moscow show trials and other atrocities. When presented with facts about Stalin, by every measure as bad, or worse, than Hitler, FDR said, "I just have a hunch that Stalin is not that kind of man. Harry [Hopkins] says he's not and that he doesn't want anything but security for his country, and I think if I give him everything I possibly can and ask for nothing in return, noblesse oblige, he won't try to annex anything and will work with me for a world of democracy and peace."

It didn't work out that way, and contrary to Gallagher, the physically and emotionally crippled, mentally incompetent FDR did in fact acquiesce in the Soviet takeover of Eastern Europe without a struggle. FDR said "it was the best I could do," and for Gallagher, "he was the only one who could have done it at all." This ignores another dynamic in play.

One of Stalin's most ardent admirers was Walter Duranty of the *New York Times*, whose cover-up of Stalin's forced famine in the Ukraine, which claimed millions of victims, played a role in U.S. recognition of the Soviet Union. Duranty had lost a leg in a train accident but as fellow Moscow correspondent Malcolm Muggeridge recalled, "he was very agile at getting about with an artificial one." One of Duranty's favorite sayings was "I put my money on Stalin," and as Muggeridge explained, "in justifying Soviet brutality and ruthlessness, Duranty was in some way getting his own back for being small, and losing a leg." The appeal of regimes like Stalin's and Hitler's is that "they compensate for weakness and inadequacy."

At Yalta, Roosevelt was weak and inadequate, so the best he could do was cave to the powerful and ruthless Stalin. This was all facilitated by the "splendid deception" that he was able bodied and able minded for the duration. He wasn't, so FDR was not what he claimed to be and therefore, in a real sense, a fake.

FDR died on April 12, 1945 at Warm Springs, Georgia, after only 80 days of his *fourth* term. Forty years later, Hugh Gregory Gallagher wrote, "the biographers continue this conspiracy. They simply accept the image of Roosevelt as he presented it to the public." Gallagher cites exceptions for John Gunther's *Roosevelt in Retrospect* from 1950, and Jim Bishop's *FDR's Last Year*, published in 1974.

The 1960 movie *Sunrise at Campobello*, with Ralph Bellamy as FDR, shows the onset of polio but does not dramatize the continuing paralysis or its psychological fallout. In the 2001 *Pearl Harbor*, John Voight plays FDR, shown seated, but with no hint of any disability. On the other hand, as Roger Ebert wrote, the film was aimed at "an audience that may not have heard of Pearl Harbor, or perhaps even of World War Two." Or perhaps FDR his own self.

The 2005 HBO movie *Warm Springs*, with Kenneth Branagh as FDR, begins with the 1920 election and ends with Roosevelt attending the nomination of Al Smith in 1928. The film focuses on Roosevelt's attempts to cure himself from the paralyzing attack but not on his effort to hide it from the public.

A president of the United States, the most powerful man in the world, issues "rules" to the press and those who claim to "speak the truth to power" go along without question. The president deploys the resources of the federal government to deceive the people. This deception enables him to stay in power, but as the deceiver grows weaker, he sells out half of Europe to Stalinist dictatorship. Even so, since 1985 nobody has bought the rights to *FDR's Splendid Deception* and put a movie on the big screen.

Back in 1985, Gallagher acknowledged that the public was uneasy about FDR's stature as a leader. "And of course," he explained, "this uneasiness, this ambiguity, has its origins in the deception practices about the president's handicap while he was in the White House and which deception is – years after his death – still being practiced."

Born in 1932, the year FDR was first elected president, Hugh Gregory Gallagher passed away in 2004. Had the intrepid author endured another 15 years, he might say that deception practices are all the rage in America.

“Native American or what?”

In her 2014 book *A Fighting Chance*, Sen. Elizabeth Warren billed herself as an “expert on economic issues” but the narrative raised some doubts.

According to the Massachusetts Democrat, born in 1949, nobody in the United States “got rich on his own.” Rather, “you moved goods on the roads the rest of us paid for” and used workers “the rest of us paid to educate.” You were safe in your factory “because of police and fire forces the rest of us paid for.” And so on, the same Big Brother economic view as the 44th President of the United States Barack Obama, formerly known as Barry Soetoro.

Not much of that dynamic emerges in Warren’s personal story, which makes it clear that, from humble beginnings in Oklahoma, she rose to a prestigious Harvard professorship through intelligence and old fashioned hard work. And like her president’s *Dreams from My Father*, Warren’s narrative also raises doubts about her own ancestral claims.

As *A Fighting Chance* explains, her father’s parents “bitterly opposed the match” with Warren’s mother because “my mother’s family was part Native American and that was a big dividing line in those days.” So they eloped. Later in the story, Warren writes, “I learned about my Native American background the same way every kid learns about who they are: from family. I never questioned my mother’s stories or asked my parents for proof or documentation. What kid would?”

Her mother’s family “lived in Indian Territory” and “her family talked about our Native American ancestry on both sides: her mother’s and her father’s families both had Native American roots.” Aunts, uncles and grandparents on her mother’s side “talked openly about their Native American ancestry.” And as Warren’s mother got older, “she spoke more forcefully than ever about the importance of not forgetting our Native American roots." So in legal terms it was all hearsay and Republicans "insisted it was all a lie. They claimed I wasn't who I said I was; they said I had cheated to get where I'd gotten." As it turned out, the critics were a more broad-based group.

The *Boston Globe* cast doubt on Warren's claims but came up with a second cousin, Ina Maples, who said "I think you are what you are. And part of us is Indian." For Warren, that proclamation settled it, but there was more to the story.

"Is Elizabeth Warren Native American or What?" ran the headline on a May 2012 article in *The Atlantic* that found no solid evidence for her claims. Warren relied on family stories, "what my brothers and I were told by my mom and my dad, my mammaw and my pappaw." And Warren cited her Aunt Bea, who reportedly complained that Elizabeth's maternal grandfather "had high cheekbones like all of the Indians do." This rather sweeping observation was also all in the family, and Warren had taken it to a new level.

The Atlantic also discovered that in 1984 Warren contributed five recipes to *Pow Wow Chow*, a cookbook, signing her contributions "Elizabeth Warren – Cherokee." So her claims were more specific than just "Native American." The piece did not reveal that the book was edited by Warren's cousin, Candy Rowsey, and that three of Warren's five recipes were fakes. As the *Guardian* noted, the Crab with Tomato Mayonnaise Dressing and Cold Omelets with Crab Meat recipes were "word for word copies of a French chef's design." A recipe for Herbed Tomatoes had been lifted from a 1959 issue of *Better Homes and Gardens*. "Great accompaniment to plain meat and potatoes meal," the magazine and Warren both say. No word whether any of the recipes came from Aunt Bea, Warren's maternal grandmother, or any specific person with high cheekbones like all Indians supposedly have.

"The longer the questions about Warren linger," *The Atlantic* piece concluded, "the harder it will be for voters to feel like they know who she really is." The questions did linger, and Warren grew weary of President Trump mocking her as "Pocahontas." In October of 2018, Warren responded with a video in which she proclaims, "Now, the President likes to call my mom a liar. What do the facts say?" Cut to Carlos Bustamante, professor of genetics at Stanford University, who says, "The facts suggest that you absolutely have a Native American ancestor in your pedigree," and Warren nods in solemn agreement. As it happened, the "facts" of Bustamante's test confirmed that virtually anybody, including President Trump, could boast as much Native American ancestry as Elizabeth Warren. And authentic Cherokees were the loudest protesters of her claims, which reporters continued to probe.

In early 2019, the *Washington Post* dug up an official 1986 Texas State Bar form, on which Warren, in her own handwriting, identified her race as "American Indian." Following this revelation, Warren apologized for identifying as Native American "for almost two decades." As it turned out, those bogus claims had been accepted and flaunted.

In 1997, Harvard Law School touted Warren as their first "woman of color" law professor, and the only "tenured minority woman" on the law faculty. It also emerged that Warren identified as "Native American" in every edition of the American Law Schools Directory from 1986-1995. In 2005, a minority equity committee at the University of Pennsylvania cited Elizabeth Warren as a minority award winner. So contrary to *A Fighting Chance*, she had deployed fake claims of Native American ancestry to advance her career. In her 2018 re-election campaign, Warren encountered an unexpected challenge.

"We don't produce enough engineers. We don't produce enough doctors. What we do is produce a bunch of scumbag lawyer lobbyists like Elizabeth Warren."

That was MIT graduate and U.S. Senate candidate Shiva Ayyadurai in Great Barrington, Massachusetts, where Sen. Elizabeth Warren was holding a meeting at the Mahaiwe Performing Arts Center. Warren told her followers to "keep pushing back" against Republicans and right-wingers. One of Warren's followers literally pushed the India-born Ayyadurai, 54, who told the crowd, "That's racism right there! You don't know what racism is. You've never experienced it." The candidate, an independent, called Warren supporters "liberal fascists" adding, "White privilege, eating your organic food while Elizabeth Warren poisons everyone else. Singing your stupid, bloody songs. Wake up, America!"

By all indications, Ayyudurai did not need to claim he was Indian to get into MIT. On the other hand, Elizabeth Warren claimed Native American heritage to help her access prestigious Ivy League institutions such as Rutgers and Harvard.

Her Republican critics "insisted it was all a lie. They claimed I wasn't who I said I was; they said I had cheated to get where I'd gotten." All that turned out to be true, and it is now easier, not harder, as *The Atlantic* put it, "for voters to feel like they know who she really is."

In the 1984 *Pow Wow Chow*, Elizabeth Warren claimed to be "Cherokee." She wasn't Cherokee, and she ripped off recipes from a French chef and a magazine published when she was ten. On the 1986 Texas Bar form, Elizabeth Warren claimed to be "Native American." She wasn't Native American, but used the false claim to advance her career. She counted on total acceptance of her claims, which would empower her to be a twofer, the first female president and the first Native American.

Investigative journalists exploded her bogus claims, but Elizabeth Warren, by all indications, believes that a longstanding record of fakery should matter not at all. At this writing, she is still running to become president of the United States, the most powerful person in the world. In October of 2019, the white Oklahoman no longer claimed to be Cherokee or Native American. On the other hand, as scandal-plagued, incoherent Joe Biden began to falter, Warren broke out a new narrative from her days as a teacher in the early 1970s.

"When I was six months pregnant, and it was pretty obvious," she explained, "the principal called me in, wished me luck, and said he was going to hire someone else for the job." Trouble was, reporters found evidence that Warren left on her own, and that the board accepted her resignation with regret. So the wealthy white Ivy Leaguer, once championed by Harvard as a "person of color," was also a fake victim of workplace discrimination.

On the campaign trail in the fall of 2019, a voter asked Warren why she wanted to defund charter schools when she sent her own children to private schools. "No," Warren replied, my children went to public schools." Trouble was, they didn't.

"Her son Alex Warren attended private schools in both Austin, Texas, and Haverford, Pa.," reported Adriana Cohen in the *Boston Herald*. So the claim was "a lie," like the notion that she was Cherokee and Native American. Even so, Warren continued her bid for the White House claiming that, unlike other Democrat candidates, she was not a socialist but a capitalist. That too is dubious.

The self-proclaimed economic expert shows little familiarity with economists such as Milton Friedman, F.A. Hayek, both Nobel laureates, and even John Maynard Keynes, who fully endorsed Hayek's *The Road To Serfdom*. Shorn of her Indian ruse, the wealthy candidate churns out boilerplate soak-the-rich rhetoric.

"Today the game is rigged – rigged to work for those who have money and power," Warren wrote in *A Fighting Chance*. "The optimism that defines us as a people has been beaten and bruised." At this writing, she is telling the world that anybody who built a successful business owes everything to the government because of public roads and fire services. Warren believes it doesn't have to be that way.

"I am determined – fiercely determined – to do everything I can to help us once again be the America that creates opportunities for anyone who works hard and plays by the rules. An America of accountability and fair play." So like Donald Trump, the fake Cherokee wants to make America great "once again." As the current presidential candidate explains:

"My story seems pretty unlikely, even to me. I never expected to run for office. I never expected to climb a mountain, I never expected to meet a president of the United States. I never expected to be a blonde. But here I am."

"EVERYTHING ABOUT HER IS A FRAUD."

On September 11, 2001, Islamic terrorists hijacked airliners and crashed them into the World Trade Center in New York City and the Pentagon. Another hijacked airliner may have been headed for the White House or the Capitol Building in Washington, but passengers forced it down and the plane crashed in a Pennsylvania field. The terrorist attacks claimed nearly 3,000 victims and the recovery efforts took a deadly toll on many others. It was easily the worst attack against the United States since Pearl Harbor, in 1941.

In 2019, first-term Representative from Minnesota calling herself Ilhan Omar gained fame for describing the 9/11 attack as "some people did something." She was born in Mogadishu, Somalia, on October 4, 1981, but has thrown up a wall around other details of her background. On the other hand, journalists David Steinberg, Preya Samsundar and others have dug up disturbing realities about the congresswoman calling herself Ilhan Omar. By many indications, the "Omar" family in whose name she entered the United States is not her actual family.

Before Ilhan Abdullahi Omar applied for asylum, her name was Ilhan Nur Said Elmi. In similar style, before the asylum application, her sister Sahra Noor was Sahra Nur Said Elmi. The United States granted asylum to the unrelated Omar family, and they allowed Ilhan, her sister and father to apply for asylum as members of that family. Ilhan and Ahmed Nur Said Elmi married in 2009 and did not divorce until 2017. In 2019, the Minnesota Campaign Finance and Public Disclosure Board found that in 2014 and 2015, Rep. Omar filed illegal joint tax returns with a man who was not her husband.

Steinberg, Samsundar and others have examined UK and US marriage records, address records, background checks of Social Security Numbers and birthdates, archived court documents and other sources. The evidence confirms that Sara Noor, Ilhan Omar and Leila Elmi are siblings with a father named Nur Said Elmi. Leila Elmi and Ahmed Nur Said Elmi lived in the same London neighborhood. Ahmed Nur Said Elmi and the woman calling herself Ilhan Omar both called Leila Elmi's children "nieces."

Minnesota attorney Scott Johnson had also investigated the woman calling herself Ilhan Omar, and that reporting came to the attention of President Trump. "As Scott reported," Trump told the crowd an October 19, 2019 rally in Minneapolis, "everything about Omar is a fraud, including her name. Scott reports his sources told him that Omar's legal husband was Omar's brother and that she married him for fraudulent purposes. You mean like coming into the United States, maybe?"

All told, Ilhan Omar's reality does not exactly square with U.S. Immigration law. In that regard, the Minnesota representative is hardly alone.

As the *Houston Chronicle* reported, Nigerian Ibraheem Adeneye, "was stripped of his U.S. citizenship after he was convicted of arranging fake marriages for others and himself." The fake marriages were intended "for the Nigerians to gain U.S. citizenship." Adeneye's previous marriage was also "fake" and he was convicted of conspiracy to commit marriage fraud, naturalization fraud, making a false statement to a federal agency and marriage fraud. His citizenship was revoked and he was subject to deportation.

Ramsi Khader Almallah, born in Jordan, paid Texas woman Rose Marie Hawley for a 1981 sham marriage. That took place four days before his student visa expired and helped the Jordanian national gain residency in 1982 and U.S. citizenship in 1988. His citizenship was revoked and Almallah, founder of the Carpet Mills chain of stores, appealed the denaturalization.

In 2007, the Fifth Circuit Court of Appeals ruled that "an alien's marrying a United States citizen for the purpose of circumventing immigration laws is not valid to confer immigration benefits." Almallah was "not eligible for immediate-relative status, permanent-resident status or naturalization," and Almallah "willfully misrepresented his eligibility to the INS at each of these stages." Therefore, "the evidence was clear and convincing that Almallah fraudulently obtained his United States citizenship," and affirmed his denaturalization. Such immigration deception, as it happens, is hardly exclusive to Muslims.

During World War II, Elfriede Rinkel served as a guard at the notorious Ravensbrueck concentration camp. After the war, Rinkel managed to immigrate to California, where, incredibly enough, she married a German-born Jew whose parents had perished in the Holocaust. Even so, she lied about her past and in 2006 agreed to leave the United States, but not before collecting $120,000 in Social Security benefits.

During World War II, Jacob Palij served as guard at the Nazis' Treblinka forced-labor camp. Palij came to America in 1949 and claimed that that during the war he worked on his father's farm. The ruse worked until 2003, when a federal judge stripped Palij of his citizenship and the next year he was ordered deported. The actual deportation didn't happen until 2018, during the administration of Donald Trump.

In 2019, the Somalia-born woman calling herself Ilhan Omar described 9/11 as "some people did something." Even so, the establishment media has been slow to take seriously the evidence of her immigration fakery. At this writing, federal authorities have not pursued the income-tax violation and mounted no case against Omar for the sort of immigration fraud that got others deported. So the often-repeated claim that "nobody is above the law," is not exactly true.

Legal immigrants and legitimate U.S. citizens might imagine Elfriede Rinkel putting on her Ravensbrueck guard's hat and running for Congress. Imagine the fake citizen claiming "some people did something," in reference to the Holocaust, or Nazi military operations against the Allies.

Imagine if Elfriede endlessly attacked U.S. leaders and U.S. policy, then attempted to portray herself as a victim of xenophobia or naziphobia. Calls would ring out for this fake to be sent back where she came from. If legal immigrants and legitimate citizens demanded such long overdue action for the politician calling herself Ilhan Omar it would be hard to blame them.

Many died, Blumenthal lied.

"A key player in the national fight against Big Tobacco," Richard Blumenthal's official Senate biography reads, "he helped bring an end to deceptive marketing aimed at children – a victory significantly lowering youth smoking rates, and compelling a multi-billion dollar settlement for Connecticut taxpayers." The senator "has successfully fought unfair utility rate charges, air pollution causing acid rain, general environmental wrongdoing, as well as a wide array of consumer scams and frauds." As a volunteer attorney for the NAACP Legal Defense Fund, "Senator Blumenthal saved the life of an innocent, wrongly convicted death row inmate who came within hours of execution."

Senator Blumenthal "graduated from Harvard College (Phi Beta Kappa, Magna Cum Laude), and Yale Law School, where he was Editor-in-Chief of the *Yale Law Journal*. From 1970 to 1976 he served in the United States Marine Corps Reserves, and was honorably discharged with the rank of Sergeant."

With Yale and Harvard in the mix, Blumenthal could boast an impressive profile and pedigree. On the other hand, the reader might wonder if the heroic life-saving, fraud-fighting Senator from Connecticut had left anything out, particularly during service in the Marine Corps Reserves.

"When we returned, we saw nothing like this. Let us do better by this generation of men and women." Thus spake Blumenthal in 2003, at a Bridgeport CT rally to show support for American troops overseas. The Connecticut attorney general implied that he had been one of those troops serving overseas. In 2008, at the Veterans War Memorial Building in Shelton, Blumenthal explained, "I served during the Vietnam era. I remember the taunts, the insults, sometimes even physical abuse." And at a 2008 event in Bridgeport to honor veterans and senior citizens, Blumenthal explained:

"We have learned something important since the days that I served in Vietnam. And you exemplify it. Whatever we think about the war, whatever we call it, Afghanistan or Iraq, we owe our military men and women unconditional support."

According to the Magna Cum Laude Harvard grad and Yale law journal editor, this was all something learned "since the days I served in Vietnam." So he knew firsthand the taunts, the insults, the lack of support. Actually, he didn't, as Raymond Hernandez pointed out in a May 17, 2010, *New York Times* feature headlined "Candidate's Words on Vietnam Service Differ from History."

As Hernandez had verified, the Connecticut Democrat "obtained at least five military deferments from 1965 to 1970 and took repeated steps that enabled him to avoid going to war."

The deferments "allowed Mr. Blumenthal to complete his studies at Harvard; pursue a graduate fellowship in England; serve as a special assistant to *The Washington Post's* publisher, Katharine Graham; and ultimately take a job in the Nixon White House."

A stint in the White House under Richard Nixon, a Republican, never showed up in Blumenthal's official senate biography, but as Hernandez showed, there was more to the story.

In 1970, with his last deferment in jeopardy, Blumenthal "landed a coveted spot in the Marine Reserve, which virtually guaranteed that he would not be sent to Vietnam. He joined a unit in Washington that conducted drills and other exercises and focused on local projects, like fixing a campground and organizing a Toys for Tots drive."

As Hernandez recalled, many politicians had fudged their activities during the Vietnam era to stay out of the war. "What is striking about Mr. Blumenthal's record," wrote Hernandez, "is the contrast between the many steps he took that allowed him to avoid Vietnam, and the misleading way he often speaks about that period of his life now, especially when he is speaking at veterans' ceremonies or other patriotic events."

One of those was the 2007 dedication of the Connecticut Vietnam Memorial to honor the 612 men from that state who lost their lives in the Vietnam war. Memorial chairwoman Jean Risley heard Blumenthal say "when we came back, we were spat on. We couldn't wear our uniforms." Risley later checked Blumenthal's military records and found he had not served in Vietnam. Even so, as Hernandez learned, the claims had been accepted with remarkable credulity.

From 2003 to 2009, at least eight Connecticut newspaper articles described him as a man who had served in Vietnam. Blumenthal was "a veteran of the Vietnam War," in the July 20, 2006 *New Haven Register* and had "served in the Marines in Vietnam." The May 26, 2009, *Connecticut Post* played up Blumenthal as "a Vietnam veteran" and *The Shelton Weekly* described the applause he received "when he spoke about his experience as a Marine Sergeant in Vietnam."

In "Just Call Him Senator," a January 6, 2010, feature in *Slate*, David Plotz described Blumenthal as "the perennial golden boy of New England politics. He's smart, handsome, and rich," and he's nicknamed "Mr. Perfect" with a "résumé makes Gore's look like a high-school dropout's."

The brilliant Harvard and Yale alum was "blessed with every political virtue except recklessness and luck." He "climbed ever upward in the '80s, winning election to the state House and Senate, marrying a rich and beautiful woman, fathering four kids, and still finding time to save an innocent man on death row."

Opponents called him "a secular saint," and "Blumenthal proved a master. Ambitious, independent, and fiercely committed to progressive activism," and so on. Then at the end readers find a May 18, 2010 "Correction" explaining:

"This article originally stated that Blumenthal enlisted in the Marines, rather than ducking the Vietnam draft, and that he was captain of the Harvard swim team. According to an investigation by *New York Times*, Blumenthal joined the Marine Reserves after receiving numerous draft deferments, and never saw combat in Vietnam. The *Times* also found that Blumenthal was not a member of the Harvard swim team, much less its captain."

The *New York Times* investigation was the piece by Raymond Hernandez, who explained, "It does not appear that Mr. Blumenthal ever sought to correct those mistakes" and he was uncertain whether he had even seen the stories. And Blumenthal could not recall the 2008 event when he told the crowd of veterans, "When we returned, we saw nothing like this."

He saw nothing like that, and he didn't return, because he wasn't there. Like his claim to have captained a Harvard swim team of which he was not even a member, it was all lies, uncritically recycled by the establishment media, proof that fake news is not a current trend.

With his falsehoods conveniently newspapered over, Blumenthal duly gained election to the U.S Senate. During the confirmation hearings for Jeff Sessions, the Connecticut Democrat charged that former New Left icon David Horowitz, author of *Radical Son, Black Book of the American Left* and many other books, was making "apparently racist" charges against Muslims. Blumenthal was unaware of Horowitz's African American family members. The senator failed to investigate any of the statements he called racist and even demanded that Sessions return an award he had received from the David Horowitz Freedom Center. David Horowitz was not present and Blumethal's gutless performance recalled the hearings for Clarence Thomas, when Democrats Howard Metzenbaum and Ted Kennedy relentlessly smeared the African American nominee.

Whether conscripts or volunteers, American soldiers fought bravely in Vietnam. Consider, for example, Marine Corps sniper Chuck Mawhinney, who took down 103 of the enemy in 16 months of duty and in a single engagement shot dead 16 Communist soldiers with 16 shots. One miss and he was a dead man.

Many others performed heroically, but the U.S. government did not give them the support they needed, and the American left, posing as "anti-war" activists, wanted the Stalinist North Vietnamese regime to win.

The Vietnam Memorial in Washington DC bears the names of 58,272 men and women who served in Vietnam, paid the ultimate sacrifice, and did not return home. Many died while Blumenthal lied.

Those who fought in Vietnam and did survive, meanwhile, can be a bit edgy about those who claimed to have served but never did so. Authentic veterans have donned T-shirts reading:

VIETNAM: IF YOU WEREN'T THERE, SHUT THE FUCK UP.

Richard Blumenthal, who said he was there but wasn't, should have heeded that advice, but no surprise that he didn't. This pampered poltroon is lucky that some actual Vietnam combat veteran hasn't smacked him upside the head, or worse. Still, it's not too late to realize that the bigger the prize, the bigger the fakery is likely to be.

LATINOBAMA REDUX

As a child, he spent time on both sides of the U.S.-Mexico border, and it isn't clear when the politician calling himself Kevin de León took up full-time residency in the United States. In the Logan Heights neighborhood of San Diego, according to one account, he lived in a house that fit 10 people into two rooms, with bare pipes running overhead and cots up against the wall. Buckets on the floor caught the water leaking from the shower above.

When Cambodian and Vietnamese immigrants began moving into the neighborhood, de León studied Southeast Asian culture in order to better relate to the newcomers. At 15 he demanded that his high school take a stand on Ronald Reagan's support of the Contras in Nicaragua. "People are suffering, because of us," he reportedly said. "We need to do something."

Kevin was reportedly the first in his family to graduate from high school, in San Diego, California. According to press accounts, he gained admission to the University of California at Santa Barbara and either flunked out or dropped out to organize illegals with the One-Stop Immigration Center. He then became an organizer with the California Teachers Association, one of the most powerful government employee unions in the state. The union man finally earned his bachelor degree from the prestigious Pitzer College, with honors according to one account. In what academic discipline he earned the degree remains unclear.

Kevin worked on political campaigns and gained election to the California Assembly in 2006 and in 2009, he failed in his quest to become Assembly Speaker. Undeterred, Kevin gained election to the state senate the following year. In 2014 the Pitzer honors grad became Senate president pro tem and promptly threw a $50,000 "inauguration" bash at the Walt Disney Concert Hall in downtown Los Angeles. As in the Assembly, Kevin's career as Senate president was undistinguished and he sometimes failed to get along with fellow Democrats. On the other hand, Californians had more to learn about their 47th senate boss.

"The name on his birth certificate isn't Kevin de León," wrote Christopher Cadelago of the *Sacramento Bee*, in a February 21, 2017, story headlined "The untold story of how Kevin Leon became Kevin de León."

On his birth certificate and voter rolls, "the 50-year-old politician is Kevin Alexander Leon." The birth certificate, not shown in the article, "says he was born on Dec. 10, 1966, at California Hospital on South Hope Street in Los Angeles. It describes his father, Andres Leon, as a 40-year-old cook whose race was Chinese and whose birthplace was Guatemala. De León's mother, Carmen Osorio, was also born in Guatemala, the document states. She was 26 when he was born." The terminology and descriptions raise some issues, but Cadelago accepted all as authentic. It was as though California Senator S.I. Hayakawa had suddenly claimed he was the descendant of a carpenter born in Scotland and journalists accepted the fabrication without a single question.

As a child, Cadelago explains, "de León spent time on both sides of the border, in Tijuana, Baja California, and Logan Heights in San Diego and identifies strongly with Mexican culture, though he doesn't know where his grandparents are from. He didn't know his father, Andres, but remembers meeting him as a boy." De León said he didn't ask his mother about him in the ensuing years, believing that "ignorance is bliss. You don't know what you don't know."

At UC Santa Barbara, "he started asking himself who he was, and whether he would be a better person if he knew the elder Leon." From that point on, he began writing "de" in front of his last name, "thinking that I would somehow connect with my father." He has used the name with the accent for 30 years but "de León never changed it on legal documents."

In Cadelago's account, "De León doesn't know where or how his parents met, but both were married and had their own families when he was born. It's unclear which countries his biological grandparents were from. De León thinks his father, Andres, was a quarter, or as much as half-Chinese, pointing to the pockets of Asian populations in Mexico, including Mexicali. He has two older half-siblings from his mother.

One recently died, he said, and the other lives in Tijuana. He also has half-siblings on his father's side, but said he doesn't know much about them. He said his mother's family lived in Guatemala and Mexico, and his mother moved to Tijuana in the 1960s."

The senate boss doesn't know when his mother relocated to Los Angeles, but "working as a housekeeper, she heard the name Kevin, and liked it. After his birth in L.A., she moved back down south, to San Diego. She married a Mexican man when de León was around five years old, taking his name to become Carmen Osorio Núñez. They later divorced. De León was raised in a blended family in a culturally Mexican neighborhood." And he "identifies strongly with Mexican culture."

Except for the strong identification with Mexico, it was a literally unbelievable story that had to be taken on faith. Unlike the case of Elizabeth Warren, investigative journalists made no attempt to document the outlandish claims of an ambitious politician. De León and his defenders made no attempt to verify the Guatemalan-Chinese ancestry through a DNA test, which would have been a simple matter. The story showed up unaltered in the senator's Wiki profile, and in leftist publications such as *Mother Jones*. Three days after the landmark *Bee* account, an action in the Senate challenged other parts of Kevin's back story.

On February 21, 2017, the Senate held a memorial for New Left icon and former California state senator Tom Hayden. Kevin de León came out as one of Hayden's biggest fans. "He was a maverick," the senate boss said. "He was an independent thinker. He was an intellectual. He was a true progressive. He dedicated his life to the betterment of our state and our great country through the pursuit of peace, justice and equity."

One senator who didn't think so was Janet Nguyen, a refugee from the Communist regime Hayden championed. Through his chief of staff, de León told Nguyen to keep quiet. The refugee wasn't having it and rose to speak. "Today I recognize in memory," she said, "the millions of Vietnamese and hundreds of thousands of Vietnamese refugees who died in seeking for freedom and democracy."

Senate Democrats shouted her down, turned off her microphone, then had the woman physically carted off the senate floor. Nobody in Sacramento could recall a smackdown like that. De León feigned outrage, pledged support for free speech, and promised an investigation that never took place.

This was a legacy of the time when Vietnamese refugees began moving into poorer neighborhoods in cities like San Diego. There they faced racist attacks from Mexicans, many in the country illegally, who regarded the Asians as intruders. This runs contrary to the account of the compassionate Kevin studying Asian history to better relate to the new arrivals. He also thought there were too many Asians in the University of California and opposed the 1996 California Civil Rights Initiative, which banned racial and ethnic preferences in state education. Prior to that voter approved measure, Proposition 209, the state had discriminated against high-achieving Asians and people of no color on the grounds that there were "too many" of them on campus. The senate boss wanted California's state colleges to ramp up discrimination once again, in defiance of the law.

After the election of Donald Trump, the senate boss explained that half his family would be eligible for deportation because they used false Social Security cards and other fake documentation. Legal immigrants and legitimate citizens had a right to wonder whether the man calling himself Kevin de León – but his birth certificate says Kevin Alexander Leon – was even supposed to be in the United States.

He authored California's sanctuary law, SB54, which protected even the most violent criminals, including murderers and rapists, from deportation. The senate boss appointed a false-documented illegal calling herself Lizbeth Mateo to the California Student Opportunity and Access Program Project Grant Advisory Committee, an official state position. As the senate boss explained, the appointee "has dedicated herself to fight for those seeking their rightful place in this country." So in the reckoning of the man calling himself Kevin de León, all foreign nationals have a right to enter the United States and hold government positions. That they vote in American elections is a matter of record.

As a State Department investigation recently discovered, a Mexican national named Gustavo Araujo Lerma applied for a U.S. passport under the assumed identity of Hiram Enrique Velez, a deceased U.S. citizen. Federal courts are charging that Araujo Lerma, 62, used this fake ID for more than 25 years and obtained legal permanent resident status for Maria Eva Velez, 64, with the help of that fraudulently obtained passport. The couple had previously married in Mexico but did so again in Los Angeles in 1992 under the fake identity. This allowed Velez illegally to gain status as the purported wife of a U.S. citizen.

The government also alleges Araujo Lerma "committed illegal alien voting" by using the identity of the late Hiram Velez in at least five federal, state, and local elections. If any election officials caught on to this voter fraud—a felony—they weren't talking. And nobody called for the State Department's Diplomatic Security Service to check all passport applications for the past 25 years to see how many belong to dead people, then cross-check the voter rolls to see how many of the falsely documented voted in federal, state, and local elections, in the manner of Gustavo Araujo Lerma.

In 2016, Hillary Clinton carried the popular vote by a count of 2.8 million and in California she received some 4.3 million more votes than Trump. California's secretary of state Alex Padilla, a close colleague of the senate boss, refused to cooperate with a federal probe of voter fraud. It was also unknown how many false-documented illegals had actually run for local, state, or federal office.

The senate boss listed on voter rolls as Kevin Alexander Leon was termed out in 2018, so he set out to unseat longtime incumbent Dianne Feinstein, San Francisco Democrat. As the race unfolded, the establishment media never challenged the unbelievable story of the Chinese-Guatemalan father the senate boss claimed he never knew. On the other hand, there were hints that something might be amiss.

Dana Williamson, who worked with de León as an aide to governor Jerry Brown, told reporters, "he's not everything he says he is." So voters had to wonder what Williamson knew, when she knew it, and why she failed to provide a more detailed explanation.

Dolores Huerta, colleague of farmworkers icon Cesar Chavez, called the candidate a "bully" and an "opportunist" and threw her support to Feinstein. The bully had been evident in Kevin de León's smackdown of Janet Nguyen, and given the victim Californians could add "racist" and "sexist" to the senate boss's resume. Huerta's charge that he was an "opportunist" was another story.

Californians could believe that this guy wanted to be the Latinobama, so he floated a story that his father was Chinese cook born in Guatemala. This was doubtless a bid to unite Asians and Hispanics the way the Illinois Democrat, who claimed to be the son of an African father and white American mother, had done with blacks and people of no color.

The man whose birth certificate reads Kevin Alexander Leon, as it does on voter rolls, was also a strident leftist who targeted Feinstein for saying that Trump might turn out to be a good president, and that it was possible to work with him. Feinstein had problems of her own, including a Chinese spy on her staff for 20 years, but voters weren't going to opt for the man who, as Dana Williamson said, is "not everything he says he is." Feinstein, still sharp at 85, thumped him 52-48.

At this writing the man "known professionally as Kevin de León," as Wikipedia explains, is running for city council of Los Angeles.

Pederast on a Pedestal

In 2019, San Francisco International Airport opened the $2.4 billion Harvey Milk Terminal featuring the exhibit, "Harvey Milk: Messenger of Hope." For the man hailed as "the first openly gay individual elected to public office in California," it was not his first tribute.

Few individuals, even among Navy veterans, get to have a ship named after them. In 2016, U.S. Navy Secretary Ray Maybus named Military Sealift Command fleet oiler the USNS *Harvey Milk*. Like the airport exhibit, that was not Milk's first honor. In August of 2009, the President of the United States awarded Harvey Milk the Presidential Medal of Freedom.

The posthumous winner, the presidential statement explains, "dedicated his life to shattering boundaries and challenging assumptions. As one of the first openly gay elected officials in this country, he changed the landscape of opportunity for the nation's gay community. Throughout his life, he fought discrimination with visionary courage and conviction."

To honor Milk's legacy, "the White House will recognize a group of outstanding openly lesbian, gay, bisexual, and transgender (LGBT) state and local elected and appointed officials as 'Harvey Milk Champions of Change.'" Observers might wonder if this champion of change lived up to his array of awards and memorials.

Born in 1931 in Woodmere, New York, Harvey Milk served in the U.S. Navy during the 1950s. According to legend, the U.S. Navy booted the sailor because of homosexuality, but there's a problem. As biographer Randy Shilts noted in *The Mayor of Castro Street*, after serving nearly four years in the Navy, Milk was honorably discharged in 1955 as a lieutenant, junior grade. So the U.S. Navy did not boot Harvey Milk for being homosexual. That was a false claim, and Milk cast himself as a victim so people will "feel sorry for me, and then vote for me."

As legend has it, Milk was murdered in 1978 by an anti-gay bigot precisely because he was an openly gay public official. That too needs examination.

Milk worked as a production aid on *Jesus Christ Superstar* and was invited to work on the San Francisco production of *Hair*. After stints in New York and Los Angeles, Milk and his partner Scott Smith moved to San Francisco. As Daniel Flynn explains in *Cult City: Jim Jones, Harvey Milk and 10 Days that Shook San Francisco*, they funded their lifestyle with unemployment checks and Milk's "political evolution from Goldwater conservative to tax-and-spend liberal corresponded with his personal evolution from taxpayer to tax taker." Milk's camera shop was insolvent but became a meeting place of sorts, and as Flynn notes, "Milk's taste in men veered toward boys."

Milk was nearly 17 years older than teenager Joe Campbell and Jack Galen was only 16 to Milk's 33. Former Marine Oliver "Bill" Sipple slept with men and "knew that Harvey Milk slept with boys." In a letter to Sipple, Milk said he had many things do that day, such as "cook dinner, fuck Jack, take a bath, fuck Jack, listen to some music, fuck Jack, wash the dishes, fuck Jack," and so on.

In September of 1975, Bill Sipple managed to stop leftist radical Sara Jane Moore from assassinating President Gerald Ford. After this heroic act, Milk proceeded to out Sipple without his consent. As Flynn notes, "Harvey Milk outed Bill Sipple as a homosexual. Bill Sipple never outed Harvey Milk as a pederast."

Harvey Milk was also attracted to Jim Jones who, Flynn recalls, "used the pulpit to extoll homosexuality." So Milk became one of Jones' most eager advocates, writing, "Such greatness I have found at Jim Jones' People's Temple." Jones responded with support for Milk's political campaigns but nothing about Jones emerges in the Oscar-winning *Milk*, a 2008 feature film starring Sean Penn.

Blue-collar Democrat Dan White, a former policeman and fire-fighter, voted with Milk to support gay issues. Supervisor White has been portrayed as a right-wing anti-gay bigot but as Flynn explains, "this isn't true." And it wasn't true that White killed Milk because he was gay.

Flynn cites supervisor Dianne Feinstein, who said "this had nothing to do with anybody's sexual orientation. It had to do with getting back his position."

So Harvey Milk was not a victim of anti-gay violence, and Harvey Milk had not been kicked out of the U.S. Navy because he was homosexual. As Flynn laments, "myths prove harder to kill than men." Besides the feature film, Milk was the subject of the 1984 Oscar-winning documentary *The Times of Harvey Milk.*

A younger Harvey Milk had been victimized by older patrons of the Metropolitan Opera, but always maintained that sexual activity was consensual and not abuse. By any standard, Harvey Milk was a pederast and it would be hard to blame gays and straights alike for outing him as a fake hero.

Likewise, Navy veterans could be forgiven for thinking that a pederast is a strange choice for the naming of a U.S. Navy ship. All veterans might wonder if the late Bill Sipple, the former U.S. Marine who saved President Gerald Ford's life, would be a better candidate for a Presidential Medal of Freedom.

The Munichian Candidate

San Diego, California, bills itself as "America's Finest City," but there's more to the place than the nearly perfect Mediterranean climate and ocean beaches. California's second-largest city is home to vast installations of the United States Navy, including training facilities for Navy SEALs. "Top Gun" pilots once earned their wings at the Miramar Naval Air Station, and U.S. Marines hold forth at Camp Pendleton just up Interstate 5.

The city and county of San Diego tend to lean Republican and the military has generated Republican candidates such as Duncan Hunter, an Army Ranger and Vietnam Veteran. Hunter served in the House of Representatives from 1993 to 2009 and son Duncan D. Hunter, a Marine Corps veteran with two tours of duty in Iraq, followed in his footsteps. In 2012, Hunter won a seat in California's 50th congressional district. As the 2018 midterms loomed, the conservative Republican faced charges for misuse of campaign funds. In that tangle, Hunter became an inviting target for Democrats, including one of curious background.

Democrat Ammar Campa-Najjar came billed as a working-class progressive, a "Latino Arab-American," "Hispanic Arab-America," and a "Palestinian-Mexican." According to the "Meet Ammar" section of his 2018 campaign website, "I was born in East County, the son of a Christian working-class mother who raised me with help from family and neighbors. From my first job as a church janitor to serving in the White House; I've devoted my life to service." Further, "as a business owner, I know the burdens we face. As a Labor Department official, I served working families."

His own family struggled and "Ammar sought work as a janitor in a church, where he later became a youth leader. He attended community college and graduated from San Diego State University, after taking time off to help reelect the president." When Ammar graduated from

San Diego State, and in what field of study, was not revealed.

In 2012, "Ammar served as Deputy Regional Field Director for the president's reelection campaign," and "following the election, Ammar secured a White House position in the Executive Office of the President. When he was unable to afford the move to Washington, DC, he secured a loan to serve on the team that selected the 10 letters that the president read every night." As someone so tight with the president of the United States, the most powerful man in the world, no surprise that Ammar Campa-Najjar went on to secure a position in the U.S. Department of Labor.

"As a Labor Department official," he writes, "I served working families." For that duty, he got his training halfway around the world: "Ammar's experience in Gaza, where he witnessed war and poverty, emboldened him to become a strong supporter of peace and economic justice."

Readers get no detail about Ammar's "experience in Gaza," a Middle East region more than 7,000 miles from San Diego and radically unlike the California city. Fortunately, Ammar addressed the subject in a November 19, 2016, *Washington Post* article headlined, "I'm a Hispanic Arab-American, and Trump's Election Does Not Shake My Belief in America."

Accordingly, "I love this country because it's a place where the ultimate comeback stories are written — including my family's own story. Only in America can the son of a Hispanic woman from the barrio and an Arab man from an occupied territory have the freedom to reimagine his life and pursue his dreams."

As the Hispanic Arab-American explains, "I spent my early years with my family under siege by American-made helicopters and F-16s that leveled entire buildings on the block where we lived. His mother, Abigail Campa, is "the modest Mexican Catholic daughter of an orphaned migrant farmworker."

On the other side, "My father, Yasser Najjar, saw both his parents gunned down right in front of him when he was only 11 years old." His father's parents are Ammar's own grandparents but he doesn't name them or explain when and where they were gunned down and why this might have happened. The narrative shifts back to the father.

"Orphaned and outlawed," Ammar writes, "my father moved across

Egypt, Lebanon and Morocco in search of a new home. On his 18th birthday, he found himself at a critical crossroads: continue seeking refuge across the Middle East, or move westward to America."

As the most casual reader would understand, nations such as Germany, France, Italy and Britain were much closer at hand, along with eastern European nations of the Soviet Bloc. Yasser Najjar wasn't looking that way. As his son explains:

"He chose America, and America chose him. In 1986, on a sunny San Diego day, my father met my mother and they soon married. In 1993, my father asked the family to relocate to the Middle East for a few years so that he could help Yasser Arafat lead a secular unity government. Today, baba is a law-abiding, taxpaying, American Muslim who has devoted his life to promoting peace between Israel and the Palestinian people. His pain was turned into purpose, to make the world a better place for his children."

Ammar does not explain why his father Yasser would choose America, the country that manufactured the helicopters and F-16 fighter jets that leveled buildings near the Najjar family. Likewise, Ammar advances no reason why America would "choose" an 18-year-old who lived as an outlaw in Egypt, Lebanon and Morocco. Readers learn nothing about Yasser's profession or trade that made him a "law-abiding, taxpaying, American Muslim" dedicated to peace between Israel and the Palestinian people. On other fronts, Ammar's memory is keen.

"I'll never forget watching my mother weep when I was nine years old. My abuelita flew from San Diego all the way to Tel Aviv to visit, only to be turned away." Where, exactly, the Hispanic Arab-American watched his unnamed *abuelita* weep remains unclear. Still, the author "vowed never to show weakness or let her see me cry. So I didn't cry when we said goodbye to our family in San Diego to live in the Palestinian territories for a few years." He didn't cry when "when we had to leave baba behind and finally return to the United States in August 2001."

Back stateside, "I didn't cry that September when 19 terrorist hijackers committed mass murder at the World Trade Center. I didn't cry that week when the Islamic school I attended was vandalized and declared unsafe to study or pray in." This might have prompted some attention from thoughtful readers.

The author counts 19 terrorists but fails to tabulate their nearly 3,000 victims, some from the plane that crashed into the Pentagon, and a field in Pennsylvania. He is attempting to establish symmetry between those attacks, carried out by Muslims, and the vandalization of the "Islamic school," that was vandalized, though he fails to name the school where he prayed and studied, or to provide the date when it was vandalized. His religious devotion at this school should establish Ammar as a Muslim his own self, just like his law-abiding taxpaying American Muslim father. Still, he laments other identity issues.

"After not being considered Arab enough in Gaza," Ammar writes, "Latino enough for the barrio, or American enough in my own country, after so many shut doors, the door to all others finally opened."

The morning after the 2012 election, "I went to work for President Obama." And as the author line reads: "Ammar Campa-Najjar, the Hispanic-Arab American son of immigrants who was born in San Diego, works for the U.S. government in Washington." How the president selected him is not disclosed, and in the end Ammar's article was like a bikini. What it revealed was interesting but what it concealed was crucial. The crucial part would not emerge from the establishment media in the United States, even as the Hispanic Arab-American set his sights on knocking off Duncan Hunter, a former U.S. Marine, in San Diego County USA.

"Grandson of Munich Massacre Terrorist is Running for Congress," headlined a February, 20, 2018 report in the Israeli publication *Haaretz*. As the story explained, Muhammad Abu Yousef al-Najjar, was a commander of Black September, the Palestinian terrorist cell that abducted, tortured and murdered eleven Israeli athletes at the 1972 Munich Olympics.

The story went viral and when the grandfather's role in the Munich murders could not be denied, the Hispanic Arab-American told reporters he had "hoped this tragedy wouldn't be politicized." He didn't use the word "terrorism" for the atrocity, and the use of "tragedy" made it seem the eleven deaths had somehow been accidental.

The beleaguered Duncan Hunter was all over it, drawing charges of Islamophobia, racism, xenophobia and so forth. Local establishment media showed little if any memory of the 1972 Munich massacre, the first terrorist attack at the Olympic games. In similar style, journalists showed little curiosity about Ammar's father, how he had managed to enter the United States, and where he might be at the present time.

Ammar claimed to be a Christian, but the establishment media did not wonder about the "law-abiding taxpaying American Muslim" father Ammar had mentioned in his 2016 *Washington Post* article, nor the Islamic school where Ammar studied and prayed before it was vandalized.

According to the *San Diego Union-Tribune*, "Yasser Najjar later moved from California to Gaza" and "Campa also lived there from ages nine to 12 before returning to San Diego just before the September 11, 2001 attacks. Why anybody would leave San Diego, "America's Finest City," for Gaza is an interesting question.

In his 2016 *Washington Post* piece, Ammar says they made the move so his father could help PLO boss Yasser Arafat "lead a secular unity government," promote peace between Israel and the Palestinian people, and "make the world a better place for children."

Little if any of that information surfaced in the run-up to the 2018 election. Duncan Hunter prevailed by a meager 3.4 percentage points. He still faced trial on the corruption charges in early 2019 but stayed in the 2020 race, challenged by several other Republicans. Ammar Campa-Najjar was also back, with an audacious new take on his grandfather, Muhammad Yusuf al-Najjar.

"I condemned him because I presumed — I accepted the premise that my grandfather was absolutely the mastermind or involved in the Munich attack," Campa-Najjar told *Newsweek* in July of 2019, "And if he was, hell, I would be the one to take him out." However, "Now, I found that it's disputed. So, upon that evidence, you can't have your beliefs immune to evidence."

As it might be recalled, the man who attended an Islamic school called the attack a "tragedy" and didn't name his grandfather, Muhammad Abu Yousef al-Najjar, who was part of it. The "evidence" that it was "disputed," came from *New York Times Magazine* writer Ronen Bergman, who contends that Muhammad Abu Yousef al-Najjar was not involved in the Munich terrorist attack, and not even part of Black September.

In 1996, a full 20 years before Ammar's *Washington Post* article, the *Post's* Barton Gellman wrote that Muhammad Yusuf al-Najjar, "was a senior leader of the PLO's Black September extremist wing. He helped plan the attack at the 1972 Munich Summer Olympics that killed 11 Israeli athletes." The February 25, 1996 article, headlined "Seeking Passage to Nationhood," included information about Ammar's father.

Yasser Najjar, then 34 and a mid-level manager in the Ministry of Planning and International Cooperation, "is proud of his father and refuses to accept that killing athletes was more repugnant than the violence of Israeli occupation over the years." Yasser Najjar explains, "he was a different generation. We will never measure up to him and people like him." Yasser thus makes it clear that his father Muhammad Yusuf al-Najjar was indeed part of the Munich massacre of eleven Israeli athletes, and by his estimation it was no worse than Israeli occupation. Despite the candor, nothing in Gellman's 3,000-word piece charts Yasser Najjar's move to San Diego, California, nor any son named Ammar who claims to have been born there on February 24, 1989.

Twenty years later, Ammar Campa-Najjar would write in the same *Washington Post* that his father Yasser Najjar "chose America, and America chose him," and that Yasser met Ammar's father "in 1986, on a sunny San Diego day." They soon married and in 1993, "my father asked the family to relocate to the Middle East for a few years so that he could help Yasser Arafat lead a secular unity government. Today, baba is a law-abiding, taxpaying, American Muslim who has devoted his life to promoting peace between Israel and the Palestinian people." All this without a word about Yasser being so proud of his father, Ammar's grandfather, for the murder of eleven Israeli athletes by the Sado-Islamists of Black September.

When Israeli weightlifter Yossef Romano fought back, the terrorists shot him, and as he lay dying, they castrated him in front of the others. The terrorists savagely beat the others before killing them. For Ammar's father, Yasser Najar, those terrorists are his version of the greatest generation.

Yasser Najjar told the *Washington Post* that the Munich massacre was no worse than the Israeli occupation. In the same newspaper, son Ammar Campa-Najjar compared the 9/11 mass murder with the vandalization of the Islamic school where he prayed and studied. Like father, like son.

The 1972 Munich terrorist massacre, Muhammad Yusuf al-Najjar's role in it, and Yasser al-Najjar's defense of it, can all be verified. The same cannot be said for Ammar Campa-Najjar's story. The scion of a terrorist royal family shapes up as a militant Muslim infiltrated from Gaza and masquerading as a Christian to run for Congress.

According to the *Los Angeles Times*, progressive Democrat Ammar Campa-Najjar has been telling voters "whether in two years, four years, or 10 years. I'm going to be your congressman one day." The bold Hispanic Arab-American doubtless draws confidence from another composite character who enjoyed great success in spite of a defining story that proved fictional.

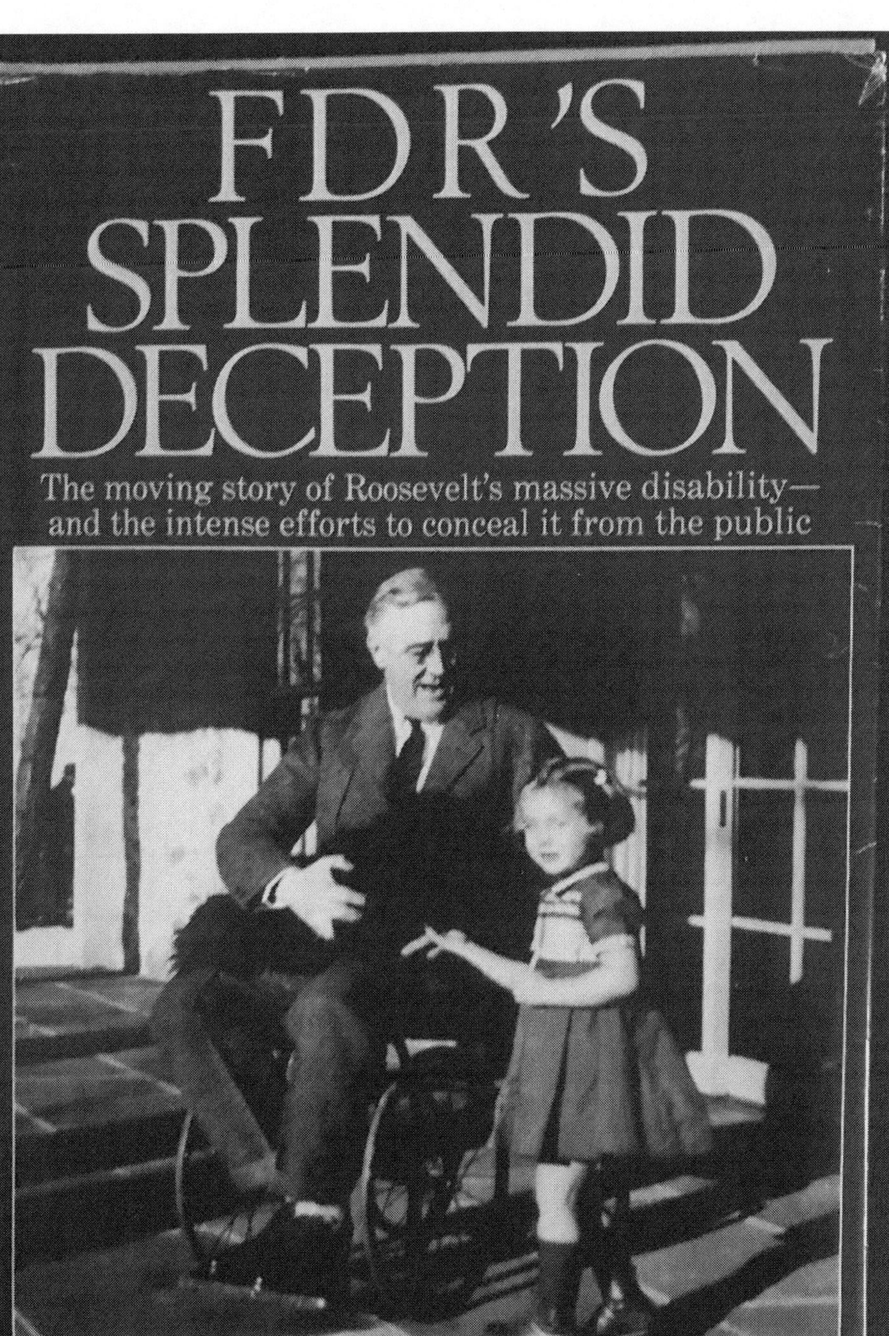

Splendid to few, a deception to many.

Not a Cherokee, as she claimed.

"Everything about Omar is a fraud."

snopes.com

Did Senator Richard Blumenthal Misrepresent His Military Serv

Did Senator Richard Blumenthal Misrepresent His Military Service?

The Connecticut Democrat admitted making false and misleading claims about his military service record but insisted he had "misspoken."

DAN MACGUILL

PUBLISHED 24 SEPTEMBER 2018

Not a Vietnam veteran, as he claimed.

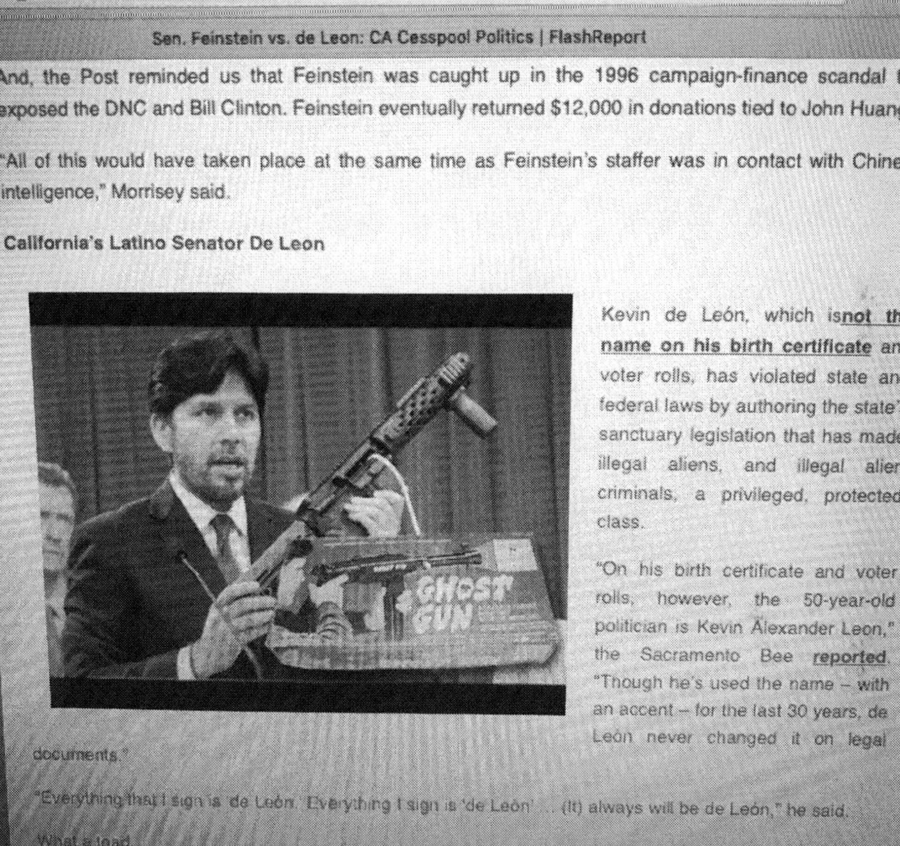

Not Secure — flashreport.org

Sen. Feinstein vs. de Leon: CA Cesspool Politics | FlashReport

And, the Post reminded us that Feinstein was caught up in the 1996 campaign-finance scandal th exposed the DNC and Bill Clinton. Feinstein eventually returned $12,000 in donations tied to John Huang.

"All of this would have taken place at the same time as Feinstein's staffer was in contact with Chines intelligence," Morrisey said.

California's Latino Senator De Leon

Kevin de León, which is **not the name on his birth certificate** and voter rolls, has violated state and federal laws by authoring the state's sanctuary legislation that has made illegal aliens, and illegal alien criminals, a privileged, protected class.

"On his birth certificate and voter rolls, however, the 50-year-old politician is Kevin Alexander Leon," the Sacramento Bee **reported**. "Though he's used the name – with an accent – for the last 30 years, de León never changed it on legal documents."

"Everything that I sign is 'de León.' Everything I sign is 'de León' … (It) always will be de León," he said.

What a load.

In 2014 I covered the many scandals in California's State Senate Democratic Caucus involving U.S. Senate candidate and Feinstein challenger Kevin de Leon.

I wrote:

- Sen. Ron Calderon, D-Montebello, was indicted on federal corruption charges in February. According

Claimed his father was a Chinese cook born in Guatemala.

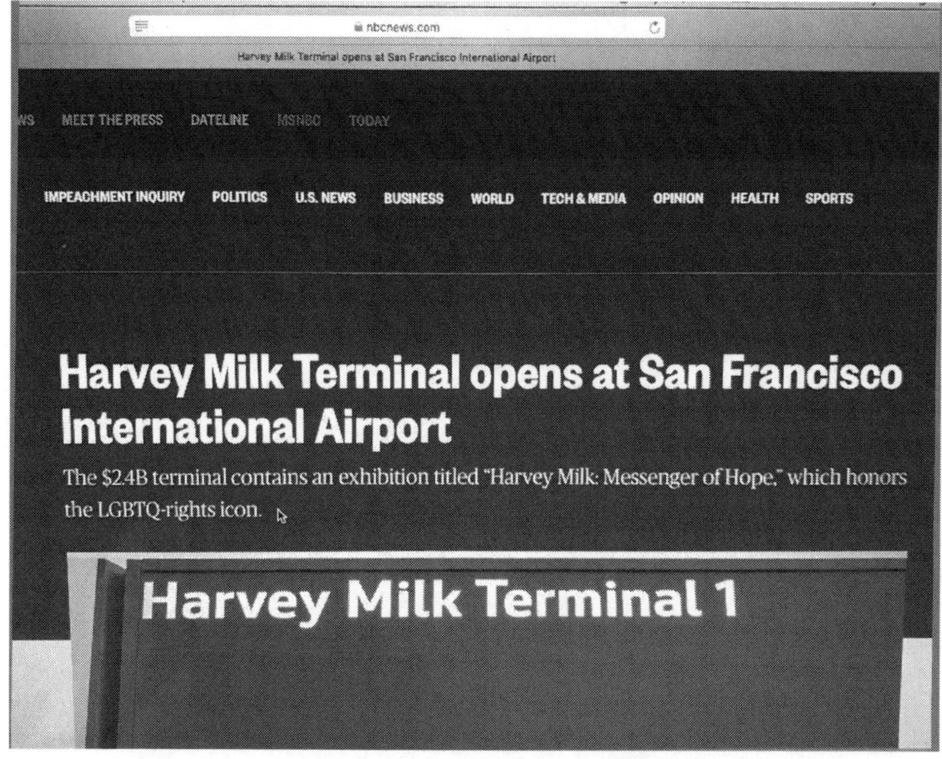

Not kicked out of Navy for being homosexual, not killed by anti-gay bigot, and never outed as a pederast.

campacampaign.com

About Ammar Campa-Najjar

A LETTER TO CALIFORNIA'S 50TH DISTRIC

My name is Ammar, the people'
was **born in East County**, the so
Christian working-class mother
me with help from family and n
my first job as a church janitor t
the White House; **I've devoted**
service.

I'm running to give back to my m
generation, and to all those seek
retire with dignity. As a business
know the burdens we face. As a
Department official, I served wo
Being your congressman isn't ab
personal politics — **it's about yo**
health, safety, and economic di

While career politicians put thei
ahead of ours and use special int
contributions and tax dollars to
lifestyles, **I'll never forget where**
I'll fight for real ethics and camp
reform – and **I won't take a dime of corporate PAC money.**

We all have a role to play in restoring America's core values: responsibility from all; opportunity for all. That
Washington, **I worked with Republicans and Democrats** to advance critical programs, including apprentice
pay double the average American's income.

Remot

A "Palestinian Mexican" descended from a Munich terrorist.

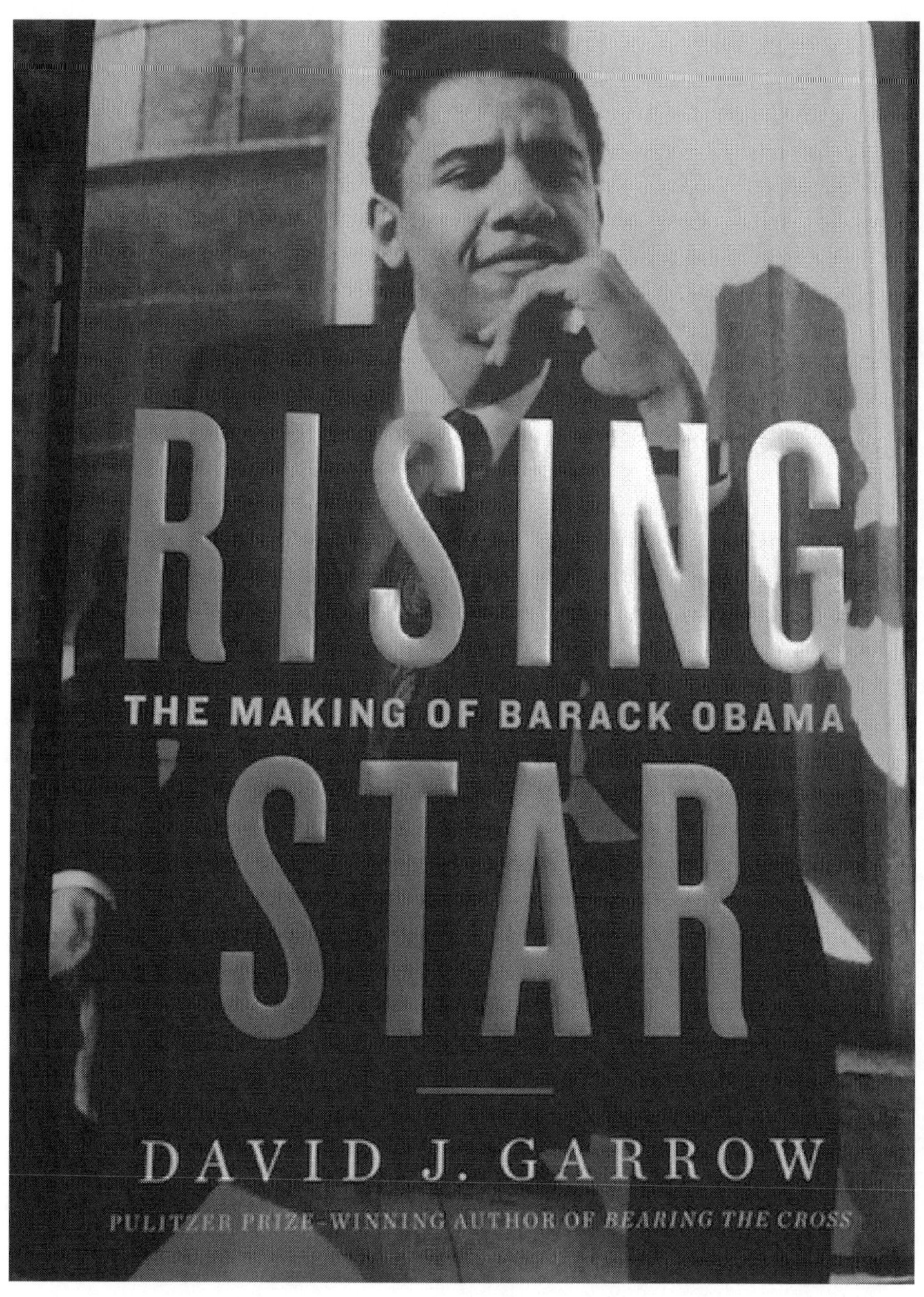

The rising star is a "composite character" in the "historical fiction" that was *Dreams from My Father*. And his defining story is "not entirely true."

President Franky Davis Jr.

> "My father was a foreign student, born and raised in a small village in Kenya. He grew up herding goats, went to school in a tin-roof shack. His father, my grandfather, was a cook, a domestic servant to the British."

That was candidate Barack Obama in his keynote address to the Democratic Party convention on July, 27, 2004. The story was based on his 1995 book *Dreams from My Father*, billed as "a story of race and inheritance." Some reviewers found it intriguing on a number of levels.

"*Dreams from My Father* was not a memoir or an autobiography; it was instead, in multitudinous ways, without any question *a work of historical fiction*. It featured many true-to-life figures and a bevy of accurately described events that indeed had occurred, but it employed the techniques and literary license of a novel, and its most important composite character was the narrator himself."

At first glance, the casual reader might think this the work of a "birther" or perhaps a right-wing journalist or Republican candidate. The reader would be wrong.

The writer is historian David Garrow, who earned his PhD at Duke University and authored, among other books, *The FBI and Martin Luther King Jr.* and *Bearing the Cross: Martin Luther King, Jr. and the Southern Christian Leadership Conference*, for which he won the Pulitzer Prize in 1986. Nobody disputes that Garrow is a writer and scholar of the highest rank, but the Pulitzer winner had some disputes of his own.

In *Rising Star: The Making of Barack Obama*, released in May of 2017, Garrow concluded that the 1995 *Dreams from My Father,* the defining story of the 44th president of the United States, was a work of fiction, which he chose to emphasize with italics. So in a real sense, the Pulitzer Prize winner was saying, the president's defining story isn't true. It featured many actual events and actual people, but the author was one of the "composite" characters. So the president of the United States from 2008 to 2016, the most powerful man in the world, was in a real sense a fictitious character. That might be enough to startle scholars, voters, and even the most casual reader.

As Garrow shows, the *Dreams from My Father* author starts out as Barry Soetoro and winds up Barack Obama, but the name on the cover is hardly the only composite character. Those intrepid readers who prevail to page 1084 of *Rising Star*, the last page of the acknowledgments before the endnotes, find this revelation:

"Barack Obama devoted dozens of hours to reading the first ten chapters of this manuscript and his understandable remaining disagreements – some strong indeed – with multiple characterizations and interpretations contained herein do not lessen my deep thankfulness for his appreciation of the scholarly seriousness with which I have pursued this project and for what became eight full hours of always-intense 'off-the-record' conversations."

Biographers do not normally let their subject review work in the manuscript stage and do not engage in negotiations about "characterizations and interpretations." As it happens, there are only ten chapters in *Rising Star*, so the subject essentially vetted the whole thing. The "remaining disagreements," may have been "strong indeed" but the scholarly Garrow does not bother to explain a single one. Maybe "Frank," who gets more than 2,000 words in *Dreams*, was one disagreement, but Garrow also charts other true-to-life characters and details missing from that book and other accounts.

Ann Dunham, mother of the *Dreams* author, married Indonesian foreign student Lolo Soetoro and the family lived in Indonesia. An unnamed "smart journalist" told Garrow that "Indonesia was *the* formative experience" for the Hawaiian-born American.

Girlfriend Genevieve Cook said of Barry that "sexually, he wasn't very imaginative" and sent him a poem:

You masquerade, you pompous jive, you act,
but clothes don't make the man,

and I know you just coverin' a whole lot of pain and confusion
You think you got it taken care of,
But I'm tellin' you bro, you don't
You masquerade, you pompous jive, you act

The man who would become the 44th president of the United States also had a three-year involvement with Sheila Jager, who had lived in Paris, spoke French and Korean "and was comfortable around the globe," just like the Australian-born Cook. Those relationships went nowhere and readers of *Rising Star* might have wondered about other people and events that failed to appear in *Dreams from My Father*. That book is not an autobiography or a memoir but an historical fiction in which the author is the most important composite character.

Was the highly regarded scholar David Garrow, with a PhD from Duke University, the first person in the world to notice fiction masquerading as biography? Did somebody know the truth and fail to speak out? And what was it, exactly, about *Dreams from My Father* that could tip off readers to the truth? Before getting into the text, they might have wondered about the cover.

Any hardcover book is an expensive proposition and book publishers tend to go with proven authors who will attract readers and ring up enough sales to earn a profit. If not celebrities or public figures, first-time authors generally have some record of publication in newspapers, magazines and scholarly journals. In 1995, if David Garrow or any critic had looked up the publication record of the name on the cover of *Dreams from My Father*, they would have found no books, no articles, no reviews, and no essays. Yet this unknown non-author calling himself Barack Obama managed to secure a book deal.

Dreams from my Father appeared in 1995 in a hardcover edition from Times Books, with a biblical epigraph from 1 Chronicles 29:15: "For we are strangers before them, and sojourners, as were all our fathers."

The cover shows a photo of an African woman with a male child seated on her lap. No man appears in the picture. The 2004 edition bears a photo of the American Barack Obama looking to his left at the photo of the African woman and her male child. On Obama's right, the cover shows a photo of a middle-aged white male in a military uniform and a female child. The man in the middle, observers might assume, somehow proceeds from the African boy and American girl in the photos.

A scholar such as David Garrow, a book critic, or any curious reader might note that *Dreams from My Father* does not indicate who took the photo of the African woman and her male child, what year it was taken, and does not identify the African woman and child in the picture. Beyond the cover, there are no photos in the book, and identity questions emerge in the foreword, as on page ix.

"I confess to wincing every so often at a poorly chosen word, a mangled sentence, an expression of emotion that seems indulgent or overly practiced. I have the urge to cut the book by fifty pages or so," says the author. "I cannot honestly say, however, that the voice in this book is not mine." That phrase might cause any reader to wince.

"I can honestly say that the voice in this book is mine," would be much cleaner, but if there was no question about the "voice" in the book, why say even that? Any reader, particularly those with the scholarly credentials of David Garrow, would recognize an authorship issue, and questions about the father.

The author saw his mother frequently and "During the writing of this book, she would read the drafts, correcting stories that I had misunderstood, careful not to comment on my characterizations of her but quick to explain or defend the less flattering aspects of my father's character."

What, exactly, the "less flattering" aspects of the father might be, and what his mother said about them, does not emerge. No scholarly reader could consult the source because the author's mother passed away in November, 1995. For his part, the author's introduction complicates the puzzle.

"We have all seen too much, to take my parents' brief union – a black man and white woman, an African and an American, at face value." As a result, "people have a hard time taking me at face value." He gives readers more reason to be skeptical when he writes, "I suspect that I sound incurably naïve, wedded to lost hopes, like those Communists who peddle their newspapers on the fringes of various college towns." Even without David Garrow's scholarly background, most readers would recognize the context.

This book was written during the early 1990s, after the fall of the Berlin Wall, the collapse of Communism, and the demise of the Soviet Union, momentous events of global importance. The most casual reader would note that the *Dreams* author shows no kinship whatsoever with the millions liberated from the various Communist regimes. But he makes it clear he's wedded to the lost hopes he associates with Communists. He is taking evasive action, and takes pains to explain it.

"I don't fault people their suspicions," the author says. "I learned long ago to distrust my childhood and the stories that shaped it. It was only many years later, after I had sat at my father's grave and spoken to him through Africa's red soil, that I could circle back and evaluate these early stories for myself. Or, more accurately, it was only then that I understood that I had spent much of my life trying to rewrite these stories, plugging up the holes in the narrative, accommodating unwelcome details, projecting individual choices against the blind sweep of history, all in the hope of extracting some granite slab of truth upon which my unborn children can stand."

At this point the scholarly Garrow, or any serious critic, might stop for review. According to the writer of this narrative, the people who have a hard time taking him at face value are fully justified in their suspicions. Indeed, the author himself has learned to distrust the stories that shaped his childhood. The narrative is full of "holes" that need to be plugged up. The author had spent much of his life trying to "rewrite" those stories and acknowledges that some details are "unwelcome" but does not explain what the details are and why, exactly, they are unwelcome.

"At some point then," the author says, "in spite of a stubborn desire to protect myself from scrutiny, in spite of the periodic impulse to abandon the entire project, what has found its way onto these pages is a record of a personal interior journey – a boy's search for his father, and through that search a workable meaning for his life as a black American."

The "stubborn desire to protect myself from scrutiny" would attract attention from any scholar with the credentials of David Garrow, any experienced book critic, and certainly the general reader. By the author's own admission, he is a man with something to hide, so much so that he proclaims a "stubborn" desire to protect himself from scrutiny.

What he has to hide must be rather serious because the author considered dumping the entire book project before finally opting to proceed. He wanted to cut 50 pages, and that is a lot of material. But now readers learn it's all about an "interior journey," and "a boy's search for his father," which hearkens back to the biblical epigraph proclaiming the father a stranger.

The author is no longer a boy in the fall of 1982, when he had just turned 21. As the narrative has it, he was "in the middle of making myself breakfast, with coffee on the stove and two eggs on the skillet" when the phone rings and a roommate hands it to him. The line is thick with static. "Barry?" a voice says. "Barry, is this you?"

The voice is Aunt Jane in Nairobi, and she uses a different name, Barry, than the one on cover of *Dreams from My Father.* So as Garrow later noted, the president who called himself Barack started out as Barry. Aunt Jane has some sad news for him.

"Listen Barry, your father is dead. He is killed in a car accident. Hello? Can you hear me? I say, your father is dead. Barry, please call your uncle in Boston and tell him. I can't talk now, okay, Barry. I will try to call you again."

This is the first mention of any uncle in Boston and he remains unnamed. Aunt Jane in Nairobi does not explain why she didn't call him herself, or why she couldn't talk more now. But she did manage to deliver the sad news.

"I sat down on the couch," the author says, "smelling eggs burn in the kitchen, staring at the cracks in the plaster, trying to measure my loss."

In a legitimate autobiography or memoir, the author would tell the story himself. Here he gets the news through an African relative with one name, the kind of exposition one would expect in a novel. So readers had good reason to flag the fictional technique more than two decades before the scholarly David Garrow acknowledged it in 2017. In the *Dreams* text, the story continues:

"At the time of his death, my father remained a myth to me, both more and less than a man."

Any scholarly critic would wonder about the use of "myth," but the author explains. "He had left Hawaii back in 1963, when I was only two years old, so that as a child I knew him only through the stories that my mother and grandparents told." As his mother explains, "Your father was a terrible driver. He'd end up on the left-hand side, the way the British drive, and if you said something, he'd just huff about silly American rules." And he was "puffing away on this pipe that I'd given him for his birthday party, pointing out all the sights with the stem, like a sea captain."

Grandma Toot, short for Tutu, meaning "grandparent" in Hawaiian, also contributes to the story. Later the author found other clues while rummaging through the closets.

"At the point where my own memories begin, my mother had already begun a courtship with a man who would become her second husband, and I sensed without explanation why the photographs had to be stored. But once in a while, the smell of dust and mothballs rising from the crumbling album, I would stare at my father' likeness – the dark laughing face, the prominent forehead and thick glasses that made him appear older than his years, and listen as the events of his life tumbled into a single narrative."

In a memoir or autobiography, readers might expect more detail than "a man" for the author's stepfather, but the Indonesian Lolo Soetoro is not named or shown. The author stared long and hard at "my father's likeness" but for some reason he does not want readers to see it. Readers get only the author's description, but the myth and the stories that needed rewriting have become a single narrative as readers learn on page nine.

"He was an African, I would learn, a Kenyan of the Luo tribe, born on the shores of Lake Victoria in a place called Alego. . . my other grandfather, Hussein Onyango Obama, had been a prominent farmer and elder of the tribe, a medicine man with healing powers. My father grew up herding his father's goats and attending the local school, set up by the British colonial administration, where he had shown great promise."

By all indications, the author is certain that the grandfather Obama had "healing powers," so he too has something of a mythical quality. Readers might expect an autobiography or memoir to include a date of birth for the father, and perhaps a name for the school. That data is missing but the author continues the scholarly theme.

The African arrived at University of Hawaii in 1959 at age 23, the first African student there who "worked with unsurpassed concentration, graduated in three years at top of his class." He also organized the International Students Association and became its first president. No documentation accompanies this claim, and the scholarly David Garrow might spot an attempt to establish a presidential pedigree. And as any reader might note, the historical fiction sometimes reads like a romance novel.

"In a Russian language course, he met an awkward, shy American girl, only eighteen, and they fell in love," the author explains. A reader might expect more detail on the mother's attraction to a man six years her senior. As the author explains, "The girl's parents, wary at first, were won over by his charm and intellect; the young couple married, and he bore them a son, to whom he bequeathed his name. He won another scholarship, this time to pursue his PhD at Harvard, but not the money to take his new family with him. A separation occurred, and he returned to Africa to fulfill his promise to the continent. The mother and child stayed behind, but the bond of love survived the distances."

Readers would expect an autobiography or memoir to provide some detail on the mother, but the *Dreams* author does not even mention her name at that point. For some reason, the author wants to protect her from scrutiny, just as he does with himself. A critic such as David Garrow could easily verify that Ann Dunham, daughter of "gramps," Stanley Dunham, was born on November 29, 1942, and died on November 7, 1995, about the time *Dreams from My Father* emerged. Here it's all about the father, but no detail on the Kenyan's first scholarship or his vaunted promise to the continent, which overrode his family concerns, nor how he might have fulfilled it. The separation simply "occurred," with no documentation, explanation, or narration of the breakup. So readers and critics alike might wonder what had actually occurred.

What stands out here is the author's claim that the Kenyan "bequeathed his name" to the American. As readers have already noted, when Aunt Jane called from Nairobi in 1982, when the author was 21, she used the name "Barry," not the name on the cover of *Dreams from My Father*. An autobiography or memoir would provide some documentation but in this historical fiction readers get nothing.

As the author explains, "there the album would close, and I would wander off content, swaddled in a tale that place me in the center of a vast and orderly universe." Like "myth," the term "tale" is certainly of interest, and the Kenyan gets more definition.

Of this storied African student, the author says, "Gramps might be struck by his resemblance to Nat King Cole, one of his favorite singers."

An autobiography or memoir would explain that Gramps is Stanley Dunham, the author's white American grandfather. The *Dreams* author fails to name Gramps and even to quote him directly. Gramps is not stating, "You know, this Kenyan student sure looks like Nat King Cole." The author is saying this is a comparison Gramps "might" make. But then, Gramps might not.

Nat King Cole (1919-1965) was a gifted jazz pianist, easily in Art Tatum or Oscar Peterson's class, who became a hugely popular vocalist in the 1950s and 1960s, with a television show to boot. But Cole, once one of the most recognizable figures in the nation, bears little resemblance to the bespectacled, pipe-smoking African student who showed up at the University of Hawaii in 1959. An autobiography or memoir might include photos of the two men side by side, enabling readers to make their own comparison. *Dreams from My Father* includes no photo section at all, which one would expect for the fictitious account David Garrow described with all its composite characters, including the author.

Stanley Dunham, the author's maternal grandfather, is an interesting character. Gramps is supposedly a humble furniture salesman but some scholars have spotted evidence of intelligence connections in his Army background. None of this emerges in *Dreams from My Father*. A scholarly critic could verify that Dunham passed away in 1992 but the author remembers him well. One day some tourists mistook his grandson for a Hawaiian, and Gramps told them "that boy happens to be my grandson, his mother is from Kansas, his father is from the interior of Kenya and there isn't an ocean for miles in either damn place."

At this point, the author's mother and maternal grandfather have both validated the story. Gramps didn't worry about race and as the author explains: "In the end I suppose that's what all the stories of my father were really about. They said less about the man himself than about the changes that had taken place in the people around him, the halting process by which my grandparents' racial attitudes had changed. The stories gave voice to a spirit that would grip the nation for that fleeting period between Kennedy's election and the passage of the Voting Rights Act."

So "the nation" is not Kenya but the United States of America. The stories about his father were "really" about "the seeming triumph of universalism over parochialism and narrowmindedness, a bright new world where differences of race or culture would instruct and amuse and perhaps ennoble. A useful fiction, one that haunts me no less than it haunted my family, evoking as it did some lost Eden that extends beyond mere childhood." In 1995, 2008 or 2017, plenty to ponder here for scholars, critics and general readers alike.

The reader has heard stories about the Kenyan father of the Luo tribe who met the shy, American girl in Russian class and the two fell in love. Now the author explains what all the stories were "really" about, and it has nothing to do with Africa or romance. It's all about the sixties in America, John Fitzgerald Kennedy, the Voting Rights Act, and some lost Eden. For any scholar, that would raise serious questions.

Within the first 25 pages of *Dreams from My Father*, before the end of the "Origins" chapter, the author raises serious questions whether the voice in the book is his own. As he explained, "I cannot honestly say, however, that the voice in this book is not mine."

The author has something to hide, and writes of a stubborn desire to protect himself from scrutiny. He tells readers why they are fully justified in not taking him at face value. In that short space readers encounter "myth," "tales" and now the prospect of the father as a "useful fiction." So nearly a quarter century before David Garrow's *Rising Star*, the author concedes that his narrative is fictional, and he has more in store on this theme.

"There was only one problem: My father was missing. He had left paradise, and nothing that my mother or grandparents told me could obviate that single, unassailable fact. Their stories didn't tell me why he had left. They couldn't describe what it might have been like had he stayed. Like the janitor, Mr. Reed, or the black girl who churned up dust as she raced down a Texas road, my father became a prop in someone else's narrative. An attractive prop – an alien with the heart of gold, the mysterious stranger who saves the town and wins the girl – but a prop nonetheless."

In a single paragraph of *Dreams from My Father*, the author uses "prop" three times. The father became "a prop in someone else's narrative," though the author did not identify the "someone else" who was spinning the narrative. The father was "an attractive prop" with his heart of gold and so forth, "but a prop nonetheless." In the next paragraph the story gets better.

"I don't really blame my mother or grandparents for this," the author says. "My father may have preferred the image they created for him – indeed, he may have been complicit in its creation."

So he was more than a prop. He "may" have preferred the image created for him, and he "may" have been complicit in the myth his mother and grandparents created. That would be the tale, the useful fiction, and he may have wanted to be a prop in someone else's narrative. The author isn't sure, and he is short on documentation.

"In an article published in the *Honolulu Star-Bulletin*," the author says, "he appears guarded and responsible, the model student, ambassador for his continent. He mildly scolds the university for herding visiting students into dormitories and forcing them to attend programs designed to promote cultural understanding – a distraction, he says, from the practical training he seeks. Although he hasn't experienced any problems himself, he detects self-segregation and overt discrimination taking place between the various ethnic groups and expresses wry amusement at the fact that 'Caucasians' in Hawaii are occasionally at the receiving end of prejudice. But if his assessment is relatively clear-eyed, he is careful to end on a happy note: One thing other nations can learn from Hawaii, he said, is the willingness of races to work together toward common development, something he has found whites elsewhere too often unwilling to do.

"I discovered this article, folded away among my birth certificate and old vaccination forms, when I was in high school. It's a short piece with a photograph of him. No mention is made of my mother and me, and I'm left to wonder whether the omission was intentional on my father's part, in anticipation of his long departure. Perhaps the reporter failed to ask personal questions, intimidated by my father's imperious manner; or perhaps it was an editorial decision, not part of the simple story that they were looking for. I wonder, too, whether the omission caused a fight between my parents."

The narrator of this tale has a lot going on here.

A scholar such as David Garrow, or any serious critic, could verify that on Wednesday, June 20, 1962, the *Honolulu Star Bulletin* published "Kenyan Student Wins Fellowship." The page-seven story with no byline reads:

> A University of Hawaii student, Barack H. Obama of Kenya, Africa, has been awarded a graduate faculty fellowship in economics at Harvard University.
>
> Obama, who began his studies at the university here three years ago, has been a straight "A" student. An economics major, he will study at Harvard for a Ph.D. in economics.
>
> He plans to return to Africa and work in economic development of underdeveloped areas and international trade at the planning and policy-making levels.
>
> A 1962 graduate, he leaves next week for a tour of Mainland universities before entering Harvard in the fall.

The scant 96 words include not a single quote from the Kenyan and nothing at all about meeting a shy American girl in Russian language class, falling in love and getting married. That is the kind of romantic international story newspapers love, but readers find not a trace of it here. The author of *Dreams from My Father* did not quote directly from the article but said the Kenyan carried on at length in rather grandiose style, representing his continent, chiding the school, expressing amusement and upholding Hawaii as a model of races working together, which he found whites elsewhere unwilling to do. That would take a lot more than 96 words. None of that is in the article and no photograph of the Kenyan accompanies the text, as the author claimed it did.

Book publishers, like newspaper editors, are well aware that their mistakes get printed. That hurts their credibility with readers, and their bottom line, so publishers do their best to keep errors to a minimum by employing editors and fact checkers. As scholars and critics would note, no such fact checker or editor appears to have asked the author for the date, author, or headline of the *Honolulu Star-Bulletin* article. For his part, the author attributes the absence of his parents in the story to a lapse by the unnamed reporter, and as he explains, the couple was "not part of the simple story they were looking for." On the other hand, readers would note, maybe the article is not the complex story the author was looking for.

A photo of the article as printed would have made an illustration of some consequence. So would the birth certificate the author says he found with the article. Why he didn't already have his birth certificate, or why it was tucked away with some press clippings and vaccination records, is not explained. A photo of the birth certificate, in particular, would be a great opportunity for the author to show that the African Barack Obama, the Kenyan foreign student of unsurpassed concentration, is indeed his father as a matter of unassailable fact. Without documentation, the claim that the Kenyan "bequeathed his name" to the American is nothing more than a "useful fiction," which David Garrow eventually concluded about the entire book and the "composite character" named as the author.

In the *Dreams* story, the brilliant Kenyan student meets the shy awkward American girl in Russian class and they fall in love. Contrast that with the account of the time the family lived in Indonesia, "the result of my mother's marriage to an Indonesian named Lolo, another student she met at the University of Hawaii." Critics would expect a legitimate memoir or autobiography to provide the stepfather's full name, but all they get is Lolo, which means "crazy" in Hawaiian and according to the author amused Gramps no end.

A critic such as David Garrow could verify that Lolo Soetoro was born in Bandung, Indonesia, in 1935, so he was seven years older than Ann Dunham. No word whether they just "fell in love," as with the brilliant Kenyan, and no word of their marriage in March of 1965. The couple divorced in 1980 but the author provides no detail of the cause. Readers would expect an autobiography or memoir to include such information, but the author has already labelled his account a "useful fiction" and explains "I cannot honestly say, however, that the voice in this book is not mine."

Readers do learn that the author's mother, who calls him "Barry," had a faith "she refused to describe as religious." In fact, her experience told her it was "sacrilegious." It was "a faith that rational, thoughtful people could shape their own destiny. . . She was a lonely witness for secular humanism, a soldier for the New Deal, Peace Corps, position-paper liberalism." Further, "She had only one ally in all this, and that was the distant authority of my father." This father is not Lolo, the Indonesian student his mother actually married. It's the elusive Kenyan, the prop in someone else's narrative.

"Increasingly she would remind me of his story, how he had grown up poor, in a poor country, in a poor continent," with a life as hard as anything Lolo might have known. According to his mother, "he had led his life according to principles that demanded a different kind of toughness, principles that promised a higher form of power."

Scholarly critics would note that information about the father comes through the mother, not directly from the author. Like Gramps, a scholarly critic might wonder which "principles," exactly, the author has in mind. He fails to name a single one, or show where these principles were in operation anywhere in the world. Scholarly critics, in particular, might wonder about this "higher form of power." Those who wonder, "higher than what?" and "over whom?" get no answer, but other issues appear to be set in stone.

"I would follow his example, my mother decided. I had no choice. It was all in the genes."

As the most casual reader would note, this author shows not a trace of the rebellion that prompted millions of other young Americans to rebel against the political and social views of their parents, and to defy their parents' plans for their career in favor of their own.

The author of *Dreams from My Father*, on the other hand, is utterly obedient and unquestioning. The decision was on his mother, that shy American girl who fell for the Kenyan student in Russian language class. Beyond the genetic determinism, readers get some physical details about the Kenyan.

"You have me to thank for your eyebrows," the mother says, "your father has these little wispy eyebrows that don't amount to much. But your brains, your character, you got from him."

Again the details come from the mother, not the author, as one would expect in a memoir or autobiography. Had the author included a photo of the Kenyan, readers could have verified that his eyebrows were not exactly wispy. And despite what Gramps might have thought, the Kenyan does not look like Nat King Cole. This author, who has a stubborn desire to protect himself from scrutiny, does not trust readers to assess a key character's appearance for themselves.

Meanwhile, back in Hawaii, the author gets into the prestigious Punahou school, explaining on page 58, "I was considered only because of the intervention of Gramps's boss, who was an alumnus."

As critics would note, he got brains and character from his father, but his admission to the Punahou school had nothing to do with stellar grades and as the author explains, "my first experience with affirmative action, it seems, had little to do with race."

The author does not name the influential boss and fails to tell readers what Gramps does for a living. Readers do learn that the author is clearly well connected and the family is not exactly hurting financially. At the Punahou school other revelations ensue.

"I thought your name was Barry," says homeroom teacher Miss Hefty. "Would you prefer we called you Barry?"

Readers have already learned that Aunt Jane was using "Barry" in her 1982 telephone call, when the author was 21, to announce the Kenyan father's death. In this scene, long before he turned 21, the student has something else in mind.

"Barack is such a beautiful name," Miss Hefty says.

As critics such as David Garrow would note, the author now claims for himself the name the Kenyan "bequeathed" to him, even though everybody else calls him Barry. In this "useful fiction" narrative, the details come from the teacher.

"Your grandfather tells me your father is Kenyan. I used to live in Kenya, you know. Teaching children just your age. It's such a magnificent country. Do you know what tribe your father is from?" The ten-year-old said "Luo." A redheaded girl wanted to touch his hair and "a ruddy-faced boy asked me if my father ate people." At home, Gramps says, "isn't it terrific that Miss Hefty used to live in Kenya?" Later in the school year, the student addresses some boys at lunch.

"My grandfather, see, he's a chief," he says. "It's sort of like the king of the tribe, you know. . . Like the Indians. So that makes my father a prince. He'll take over when my grandfather dies." As the author explains "a part of me really began to believe the story. But another part of me knew that what I was telling them was a lie, something I'd constructed from the scraps of information I'd picked up from my mother."

Even without the scholarly credentials of David Garrow, readers find a lot going on here.

By page 63 the author of *Dreams from My Father*, has added "lie" to such terms as "myth," "tale," "useful fiction," and "prop." And the author says he preferred the father's more distant image "an image I could alter on a whim or ignore when convenient." His father "remained something unknown," even though his mother had explained about his hard life in a poor continent, his principles that promised a higher form of power, and how he got his brains and character from him. The mother had also explained how it was in his genes that he would follow him, and that he had no choice in the matter. His mother had maintained a correspondence with the distant father throughout the time they had been in Indonesia, and "he knew all about me." Like his mother, his father had remarried, "and I now had five brothers and one sister living in Kenya."

So in this useful fiction, the Kenyan Barack H. Obama had, count 'em, six children. With that kind of responsibility, bolting for Hawaii to visit the American woman who gave birth to his child must have been quite an operation, especially since the woman was now married to the Indonesian Lolo Soetoro. Even so, the father was coming to Hawaii to visit – for a full month.

"He was much thinner than I expected," the author explains, "the bones of his knees cutting the legs of his trousers in sharp angles." The Kenyan wore a blue blazer, white shirt and a scarlet ascot. There was "a fragility about his frame" and he carried a cane with a "blunt ivory head." When he took off his horned-rimmed glasses the eyes are yellow, "the eyes of someone who has had malaria more than once."

Readers find plenty of detail here, and medical knowledge on malaria, but the character seems something of a composite, just like the author, as David Garrow discovered. The blue, white and red clothing evokes the Union Jack or American stars and stripes more than any sort of African style. No mention here of Gramps saying the fellow looked like Nat King Cole, though that was something Gramps "might" say.

The Kenyan gave his son three wooden figurines "a lion, an elephant and an ebony man in tribal dress beating a drum," all items commonly purchased by tourists. The Kenyan explains, "they are only small things." Maybe he meant that his son could expect bigger and more meaningful things during the month-long visit.

"There was so much to tell in that single month, so much explaining to do; and yet, when I reach back into my memory for the words of my father, the small interactions or conversations we might have had, they seem irretrievably lost."

People who knew the Kenyan Barack Obama consistently describe him as verbose and opinionated. Here the author of *Dreams from My Father* can't remember a single statement this big-time talker made during an entire month. It was all "irretrievably lost," like those 18 minutes on the Nixon tapes, the continent of Atlantis, or the corpse of Jimmy Hoffa.

Coming so soon after the author added "lie" to "myth" and other evasive language, scholar, critics and general readers had grounds to believe that this too was false, and part of that "useful fiction," a mere prop in someone else's narrative, as the author also said. He can't explain the irretrievable loss, but his wife, whom he does not name, says boys and their fathers don't always have much to say to each other unless and until they trust. Indeed, the author says, "I often felt mute before him, and he never pushed me to speak." That part the author remembers, along with the yellow eyes of someone who had malaria more than once. Before he departed back to Africa, the father was coming to speak in Miss Hefty's class.

"We have a special treat for you today," Miss Hefty says. "Barry Obama's father is here, and he's come all the way from Kenya, in Africa, to tell us all about his country."

As critics would note, the teacher who has already proclaimed Barack a beautiful name, is now using the Obama surname the Kenyan supposedly "bequeathed" to the author. She is not using Soetoro, which was in fact the surname of the Indonesian student his mother had married. Here is how the appearance went down, according to the author, on page 69 of *Dreams from My Father*.

"He was leaning against Miss Hefty's thick oak desk and describing the deep gash in the earth where mankind had first appeared. He spoke of the wild animals that still roamed the plains, the tribes that still required a young boy to kill a lion to prove his manhood. He spoke of the customs of the Luo, how elders received the utmost respect and make laws for all to follow under great-trunked trees. And he told us of Kenya's struggle to be free, how the British had wanted to stay and unjustly rule the people, just as they had in America; how many had been enslaved only because of the color of their skin, just as they had in America, but that Kenyans, like all of us in the room, longed to be free and develop themselves through hard work and sacrifice."

As readers learn, the student who could not remember a single thing the Kenyan said in a full month now shows incredible recall. On the other hand, like the four-paragraph article in the *Honolulu Star-Bulletin*, the account includes not a single direct quotation from the man the author described to his pals at the prestigious Punahou school. After his father spoke, Miss Hefty was "absolutely beaming with pride" and classmates asked his father questions, "each of which my father appeared to consider carefully before answering." The author gives no detail on the questions, perhaps about that deep gash in the earth where mankind first appeared, or his father's answers. Even so, plenty here for all readers to ponder.

The *Honolulu Star-Bulletin* had seen fit to note the Kenyan's departure from the islands for Harvard in 1962. The Kenyan's return some ten years later to address a class at the prestigious Punahou school is the kind of story newspapers love, but the *Star-Bulletin* apparently showed no interest. Perhaps that was the fault of the same reporter who failed to mention the author and his mother in 1962. Or perhaps not.

"You've got a pretty impressive father," a certain Mr. Eldridge tells the author. In similar style, the ruddy-faced boy who had asked about cannibalism said "your dad is pretty cool," a direct quote. The author has plenty of quotes from Gramps, grandma Toot, and others, but not a single quote from the time his Kenyan father showed up in the classroom of Miss Hefty, a teacher who had lived in Kenya. Any kid of ten would tend to remember a thing like that, but maybe this too was irretrievably lost.

In the next two weeks, the author explains, father and son posed for pictures, "the only ones I have of us together, me holding an orange basketball, his gift to me, him showing off the tie I've bought him." No word about the pipe the author says he bought him for his birthday, but the tie prompts the Kenyan to say, "Ah, people will know that I am very important wearing such a tie."

That's a direct quote, so an astute reader might believe that all the memories of the visit are not irretrievably lost after all. The author managed to retrieve at least one. On the other hand, maybe the photos are lost because neither one shows up in *Dreams from My Father*, which has no photo section. Given the novelistic style of the "useful fiction," a scholarly critic might wonder if the photos ever existed, and if the visit ever took place.

As the author has it, father and son go to a Dave Brubeck concert, of which the son provides no details of personnel, venue, or compositions performed. A scholarly critic might find an existential problem with this gig. The classic Dave Brubeck quartet with Paul Desmond, Joe Morello and Eugene Wright disbanded at the end of 1967. The author is writing about 1971, when Brubeck lost his recording contract with Columbia, not exactly the ticket to extensive touring, which often takes place to promote a new album. Brubeck had suffered an injury diving in the surf in Hawaii but that was in 1951.

Jazz is "an American musical art form. No America, no jazz," as Jazz Messengers drummer Art Blakey said after living for a time in Africa. "I've seen people try to connect it to other countries, for instance to Africa," Blakey said, "but it doesn't have a damn thing to do with Africa." So the Kenyan student would be unlikely to show much knowledge about jazz. And any reader of *Dreams from My Father* would note what the Kenyan breaks out on the day of his departure: two 45-RPM records, "in dull brown dust jackets."

"Barry! Look here," the Kenyan says. "I forgot that I had brought these for you. The sounds of your continent."

So as readers note, the African father, who worked with "unsurpassed concentration" and graduated at the top of his class in three years, also suffers from some memory issues. The Kenyan evidently forgot to give his son Barry the 45 RPM records upon arrival, when he gave him the wooden carvings of the lion, elephant and the ebony man in tribal dress beating a drum. And according to the "useful fiction" narrative, the African even failed to break out the records at Christmas. Perhaps to compensate, he now fires up his grandparents' old stereo. The music wasn't "Take Five," the Paul Desmond composition made famous by the Brubeck quartet, or the great John Coltrane's "Giant Steps," or any jazz composition. As Bob Seger might have said, it was that old fashioned rock and roll.

"A tinny guitar lick opened," the author writes, "then the sharp horns, the thump of drums, then the guitar again, and then the voices, clean and joyful as they rode up the back beat, urging us on."

As a scholarly critic might note, the author fails to name the tune or identify the recording artists. Kids tend to remember things like that, but maybe that too was irretrievably lost. On the other hand, the scene brims with detail and dialogue.

"Come, Barry," my father said. "You will learn from the master." And "suddenly his slender body was swaying back and forth" and, the author says, "I took my first tentative steps."

The pipe-puffing yellow-eyed African, who looked frail and carried a cane, was suddenly transformed into a cross between Chubby Checker, famous for "the Twist," and Edwin Starr's Agent Double-O Soul, who could do "the Twine and the Jerk." As readers would recall, this was an African whose "image I could alter on a whim or ignore when convenient." At this point, the scholarly critic might conduct some review.

The Kenyan was not quoted in the June 20, 1962 article in the *Honolulu Star-Bulletin,* which does not say what the author says it did, and does not include the photo he claimed was there. Likewise, the author had no quotes from the Kenyan's appearance in Miss Hefty's class. Over a full month with his father, the man of unsurpassed concentration from whom he got his brains and his character, he can't remember a single thing the Kenyan said. It's all irretrievably lost, except it isn't.

The author is at pains to tell the reader that father and son went to a Dave Brubeck concert. And he remembers what his father told the son about "the sounds of your continent" and how the master hoofer boogied about the room on the day he departed back to Africa, from whence he came, to fulfill "his promise to the continent," whatever that was. For any reader or critic who had been paying attention, none of this would be strange.

The African was a prop in someone else's narrative, altered or ignored as the occasion demands. Interactions father and son "might" have had over an entire month are irretrievably lost. The author talks up the myth, the tale, the prop, the lie, and the useful fiction. He says people have trouble taking him at face value and confirms that their suspicions are justified. All this comes before introduction of the useful fiction's most interesting character.

On page 76 of *Dreams from My Father*, the author introduces "a poet named Frank who lived in a dilapidated house in a run-down section of Waikiki. He had enjoyed some modest notoriety once, was a contemporary of Richard Wright and Langston Hughes during his years in Chicago – Gramps once showed me some of his work anthologized in a book of black poetry. But by the time I met Frank he must have been pushing eighty, with a big dewlapped face and an ill-kempt gray Afro that made him look like an old, shaggy lion."

The book includes no last name or photo of the poet named Frank, and Gramps does not say he looks like Nat King Cole, Louis Jordan, Joe Louis, or any other African American of note. On the other hand, Frank's connections to Richard Wright and Langston Hughes would spark the interest of any serious critic. And it could be easily verified that the *Dreams* author, who has that stubborn desire to protect himself from scrutiny, helpfully identified Frank. On September 20, 1995, in a televised speech at the Cambridge library, the author clearly identified the poet as "Frank Marshall Davis." In the age of the Internet, any reader or critic could easily verify that Frank did enjoy more than a modest notoriety.

In *Livin' the Blues: Memoirs of a Black Journalist and Poet* (University of Wisconsin Press, 1992) Davis proudly notes his inclusion in *Who's Who in the Midwest* and *Who's Who in America*. Even cursory research would confirm that Frank is completely candid about being a Communist, and Frank makes it clear that he joined the Communist Party after the Hitler-Stalin Pact, when many others departed, never to return.

A critic such as David Garrow, familiar with American Communism, would know that Davis joined a white-led Communist Party that did not regard blacks as Americans and had mapped out a separate homeland for blacks in the south.

In Chicago, Davis worked with Vernon Jarrett of the Council of American Youth for Democracy, a Communist Party front group and a kind of Stalin Youth chapter. Frank also worked with Jarrett on the Citizens Committee to Aid Packinghouse Workers. Frank served on the board of the Chicago Civil Liberties Committee with his fellow

Stalinist Paul Robeson and a man named Robert R. Taylor. None of this emerges in *Dreams from My Father*, nor the reason Frank, who enjoyed all that notoriety in Chicago, suddenly moved to Hawaii.

The Communist Party USA was a wholly owned subsidiary of the Soviet Union and like all national Communist parties managed through the Communist International, the Comintern, in Moscow. Party members were under strict discipline and like the inmates of Communist nations, not at liberty to do their own thing. In 1948 the Party shipped Davis to Hawaii, not yet a state and a major target of Stalin's post-war expansionism. In that cause, Frank wrote for *Honolulu Record*, a publication backed by the CPUSA and the International Longshoremen's and Warehousemen's Union, headed by Harry Bridges, another Communist and Soviet agent. Davis' journalism was the same pro-Soviet boilerplate. He blasted opponents as fascists, racists, Ku Kluckers, Nazi storm troopers and so on. His primary political targets were Democrats, particularly U.S. President Harry Truman.

Frank Marshall Davis was a photography enthusiast and in his first year in Hawaii, he deployed a telephoto lens to take shots of remote Hawaiian beaches. So it was not for nothing that Davis wound up on the FBI's Security Index. This meant that in the event of war, he would have been arrested immediately. Frank Marshall Davis' FBI file runs 600 pages, longer than *Dreams from My Father* and *Livin' the Blues*, and was only made available in recent times.

Pulitzer Prize winner David Garrow, who wrote of "the making of Barack Obama," is knowledgeable about American Communism but *Dreams* may have prompted more research.

The author devotes more than 2,000 words to Frank, who later develops an existential problem. Frank disappears in the audio edition of *Dreams* and appears not at all in *The Audacity of Hope* in 2006. Neither is Frank mentioned in *Believer*, the 2015 book by White House advisor David Axelrod, proclaimed "Obama's narrator" by the *New York Times*. In similar style, *The World As It Is, A Memoir of the Obama White House*, by speechwriter and national security advisor Ben Rhodes contains not a single word about Frank. That book emerged in 2018, one year after David Garrow provided some background on the true-to-life character. Rhodes praises *Dreams from*

My Father as the president's "Rosetta Stone," but fails to note that Garrow pegged it as fiction.

As Garrow writes, Frank Marshall Davis was "an African American writer of significant power and great promise, a leading voice in what would be called the Chicago Black Renaissance." His poetry did not survive his generation because it was "too polemically political." Communists had to be "artists in uniform," serving a political purpose, otherwise the Party regarded them as bourgeois purveyors of meaningless fare.

As Garrow's readers learn, Frank was on the FBI's Security Index, a register of the nation's "most dangerous supposed subversives." Frank was also on DETCOM, the FBI's "most wanted" list of top Communists marked for immediate detention in event of national emergency. He also wrote *Sex Rebel: Black*, which he said was autobiographical, and as Garrow notes, "Davis' Communist background plus his kinky exploits made him politically radioactive." This is a helpful and accurate explanation, but there's more to Frank's story.

The CPUSA organization in the Hawaiian islands was formidable but ultimately lost the battle. President Dwight Eisenhower signed the Hawaii Admission Act on March 12, 1959, and on August 21, 1959, Hawaii duly became the fiftieth U.S. state. If Frank was only the president's "mentor," as Paul Kengor contended in *The Communist: Frank Marshall Davis: The Untold Story of Barack Obama's Mentor* (2012), one doubts whether Frank would have been included in *Dreams from My Father* at all. Frank was very important to the author, who also has this stubborn desire to avoid scrutiny. So no surprise that the author decks out the Stalinist Davis in a disguise like Grady Wilson on "Sanford and Son," the kind of stereotype the CPUSA hated.

Frank, says the author, "would read us his poetry whenever we stopped by his house, sharing whiskey with Gramps out of an emptied jelly jar. As the night wore on the two of them would solicit my help in composing dirty limericks. Eventually the conversation would turn to laments about women."

"They'll drive you to drink, boy," Frank would say, "and if you let 'em, they'll drive you into your grave."

Scholarly critics such as David Garrow, and general readers alike, might notice that, unlike the Kenyan, nothing about Frank seems irretrievably lost to the author, who never hesitates to quote him directly and is obviously very fond of the man. With the Kenyan father, the author preferred a distant image he "could alter on whim or ignore altogether." In similar style, the author ignores Frank's faithful service on behalf of the Soviet Union. *Dreams from My Father* includes no quotes from Frank's journalism, a huge body of work reflecting his belief that the white European Stalinists who ran the Soviet Union were always right and represented the future.

In *Livin' the Blues*, Frank Marshall Davis wrote extensively about jazz and taught jazz history at the Abraham Lincoln School in Chicago, a Communist Party operation. Davis was not a musician and held some rather strange ideas. For example, he called be-bop an effort to make jazz "acceptable to traditional white standards." Actually, the be-boppers, all virtuoso musicians, wanted to play something that was interesting to themselves, and outside of the traditional musical structures.

Frank also worked as a disc jockey playing jazz on WJJD, a radio station owned by the multi-millionaire Marshall Field. This does not emerge in *Dreams from My Father*, which tellingly attributes the affection for jazz to the Kenyan student. In this tale it was the African, not Frank, who allegedly took his ten-year-old son to a Dave Brubeck concert and danced around the house as though auditioning for "Soul Train." As readers might recall, the African was a prop in someone else's narrative, part of the author's myth and useful fiction, and could be altered at will and ignored when convenient. So in 2017, the scholarly David Garrow was only confirming what the *Dreams* author had been saying all along.

On page 79 of *Dreams from My Father* the author proclaims that "respect came from what you did and not who your daddy was." The author's daddy was important, but not his only influence. He goes to the library and reads James Baldwin, Ralph Ellison, Langston Hughes, Richard Wright, and W.E.B. DuBois. He does not learn that Richard Wright, author of *Native Son* and *Black Boy*, was one of the authors in *The God That Failed*, a landmark indictment of Communist tyranny. He finds all of them "exhausted, bitter men, the devil at their heels," and "only Malcolm X's autobiography seemed to offer something different." One line in the book stayed with him, Malcolm's wish that the white blood that ran through him "might be expunged." That would never "recede into mere abstraction" like all that stuff about blue-eyed devils. So the author wonders "what else I would be severing if and when I left my mother and my grandparents at some uncharted border."

A scholar with the erudition of David Garrow would recognize Baldwin, Ellison, Hughes and Wright as writers of the first rank, who dealt with what is now called "social issues" such as racism, segregation and so forth. To say that "only" Malcom X offered something different might indicate the effort of a pampered American to cultivate a radical image. In this narrative, the legacy problem is not the Frank the Stalinist. It's the white folks in the author's background.

The author and his friend Ray meet a tall gaunt man named Malik, a follower of the Nation of Islam. This NOI holds that a scientist named Yakub created the white race more than 6,000 years ago on the Isle of Patmos. According to this racist belief, which is not part of Islam, Shakespeare, Tolstoy, Eleanor Roosevelt, Johann Sebastian Bach, Abraham Lincoln, Dave Brubeck, Hillary Clinton, Gramps and the author's own mother all proceed from Yakub's experiment. Maybe the author knew that then forgot it. After all, he claims to have forgotten everything a verbose Kenyan said in a whole month. A scholarly critic such as David Garrow might say the author lacks courage and is not much of a critical thinker.

"Malcolm tells it like it is, no doubt about it," says one of the guys who overheard the author conversing with Malik. This prompts another unidentified "guy" to say. "Yeah, but I tell you what. You won't see me moving to no African jungle anytime soon. Or some goddamned desert somewhere, sitting on a carpet with a bunch of Arabs. And you won't see me stop eating no ribs. Gotta have them ribs. And pussy, too. Don't Malcolm talk about no pussy? Now you know that ain't gonna work."

Scholarly critics might not know what to make of that. It reads like something from Robert Townsend's *Hollywood Shuffle*, in which white instructors teach blacks how to act black.

As he drives to the hoop, Ray says "I don't need no books telling me how to be black."

The author gets back to Frank, "sitting in his overstuffed chair, a book of poetry in his lap, his reading glasses slipping down his nose. It had been three years, the author says but "he looked the same, his mustache a little whiter, dangling like dead ivy over his heavy upper lip, his cut-off jeans with a few more holes and tied at the waist with a length of rope."

Frank pulls down a bottle of whiskey and pours drinks into plastic cups. The conversation centers on conditions back in Kansas, where both Frank and Gramps lived, and where Frank would have to step off the sidewalk to let the white folks pass by Gramps would not be eager to talk about that, and he can't know Frank the way Frank knows him. Meanwhile, Grandma Toot had evidently been frightened by a large black man, and Frank explains the dynamic.

"What I'm trying to tell you is, your grandma's right to be scared. She's at least as right as Stanley is. She understands that black people have a reason to hate. That's just how it is. For your sake, I wish it were otherwise. But it's not. So you might as well get used to it.

"Frank closed his eyes again. His breathing slowed until he seemed to be asleep. I thought about waking him, then decided against it and walked back to the car. The earth shook under my feet, ready to crack open at any moment. I stopped, trying to steady myself, and knew for the first time that I was utterly alone." Except he wasn't alone. His mother and maternal grandparents were still around, and so was Frank.

In this myth, tale, and useful fiction, "black people have a reason to hate." That squares with Davis, a prodigious hater, and the Communist Party to which he belonged is a hate group by any standard. The erudite David Garrow would know this, and also that Frank studied journalism at Friends College then transferred to Kansas State, so Davis did not lack educational opportunity and took full advantage. That casts in a strange light the advice he gives the *Dreams* author.

College, Frank warns, is "an advanced degree in compromise." And as he tells Barry,

"You're just like the rest of these young cats out here. All you know is that college is the next thing you're supposed to do. And the people who are old enough to know better, who fought all those years for your right to go to college – they're just so happy to see you in there that they won't tell you the truth. The real price of admission."

"And what's that?" the graduate of the prestigious Punahou school wonders.

"Leaving your race at the door," Frank says. "Leaving your people behind. Understand something, boy. You're not going to college to get educated. You're going there to get trained. They'll train you to want what you don't need. They'll train you to manipulate words so they don't mean anything anymore. They'll train you to forget what it is that you already know. They'll train you so good, you'll start believing what they tell you about equal opportunity and the American way and all that shit. They'll give you a corner office and invite you to fancy dinners, and tell you you're a credit to your race. Until you want to actually start running things, and they'll yank on your chain and let you know that you may be a well-trained, well-paid nigger, but you're a nigger just the same."

At this point, readers might not have been surprised if Frank said going to college was "acting white." The student wonders if he should go, and Frank falls back in his chair with a sigh.

"No, I didn't say that. You've got to go. I'm just telling you to keep your eyes open. Stay awake."

"It made me smile," the author writes, "thinking back on Frank and his old Black Power dashiki self. In some ways, he was as incurable as my mother, as certain in his faith, living in the same sixties time warp that Hawaii had created."

Readers might recall that when the Kenyan was about to return to Africa, the author decked him out in American influence with "the music of your continent." Now Frank, the card-playing, whiskey-drinking jokester who fancies himself a sage, shows the African influence as "his old Black Power dashiki self." Frank can't be ignored, but like the Kenyan he can be altered on a whim. In someone else's narrative, which is also a myth and a tale, pretty much anything goes.

The Kenyan Barack Obama jumped at the chance to attend the University of Hawaii and did not consider that decision any sort of compromise or selling out his friends and family in Kenya. If the Kenyan's American son chose the same school, that would have been quite a story for the *Honolulu Star-Bulletin*, which duly noted the Kenyan's departure for Harvard. In this tale, young Barry shows not the slightest inclination to follow the Kenyan's educational footsteps. Instead he is off to Occidental College, an upscale private liberal arts school in Los Angeles. No word whether, as with the prestigious Punahou school, family connections were the primary factor in admission. The narrator mentions no academic scholarship.

Occidental College put out the literary magazine *Feast*, and in the Spring 1982 issue the student from Hawaii known as Barry published a poem titled “Pop,” in which the subject “recites an old poem he wrote before his mother died.” So “Pop” is a poet, and as student has it:

Pop takes another shot, neat,
Points out the same amber
Stain on his shorts that I’ve got on mine and
Makes me smell his smell, coming
From me. . .

The “Pop” poem concludes:

I see my face, framed within
Pop’s black-framed glasses
And know he’s laughing too.

A scholarly critic might recall that in *Dreams from My Father*, the narrator never calls the Kenyan “Pop.” This is clearly Frank, a poet, and the author sees his own face framed within Pop’s black-framed glasses. The author has amber stains on his shorts, just like Pop, who “makes me smell his smell, coming from me.” What that might mean, exactly, invites speculation, but it’s all rather intimate and personal. Stanley Dunham was still around when the poem appeared, but Gramps is not on record with any interpretation of the work. Neither did Toot or the author’s mother publish her thoughts on the “Pop” poem, which nowhere appears in *Dreams From My Father*. The author, after all, has a stubborn desire to protect himself from scrutiny. On the other hand, at that point the student’s influences were certainly showing.

In the accounts of Occidental students and professors alike, the student Barry was a doctrinaire pro-Soviet Marxist. Nothing the author has explained about the Kenyan would indicate that kind of profile. If the Kenyan had been pro-Soviet his first choice for college would have been Patrice Lumumba University in the USSR, the socialist motherland, not the University of Hawaii in the capitalist United States. On the other hand, as Garrow recognized Frank was a pro-Soviet propagandist and proud of it.

At Oxy, as he called it, "to avoid being mistaken for a sellout," the student hangs with Marxist professors and the politically active black students. Fellow student Marcus has a run-in with the LAPD.

"They had no reason to stop me. No reason 'cept I was walking in a white neighborhood. Made me spread-eagle against the car. One of 'em pulled out his piece. I didn't let 'em scare me, though. That's what gets these storm troopers off, seeing fear in a black man. . ." The author had been "listening to Marcus pronounce on his authentic black experience." Marcus also tells "Barack" that *Heart of Darkness* is a "racist tract" that will "poison your mind." A black student named Regina, also without a last name, witnesses the exchange.

"What did Marcus call you just now? Some African name, wasn't it?"

"Barack."

"I thought your name was Barry."

"Barack's my given name. My father's name. He was Kenyan."

"Does it mean something?"

"It means 'blessed.' In Arabic. My grandfather was a Muslim."

"Barack, it's beautiful," Regina says, in the style of Miss Hefty, the Punahou teacher who had been to Kenya. But Regina is curious.

"So why does everybody call you Barry?"

"Habit, I guess. My father used it when he arrived in the States. I don't know whether that was his idea or somebody else's. He probably used Barry because it was easier to pronounce. You know – helped him to fit in. Then it got passed on to me. So I could fit in."

A scholarly critic such as David Garrow would have a hard time finding cases where the Kenyan calls himself "Barry." Earlier in the narrative, when the author explained that the Kenyan from the Luo tribe "bequeathed" his name, there was no mention of "Barry." But then, as the author says, this is someone who can be altered on a whim or ignored when convenient, the familiar prop in someone else's narrative.

The Kenyan prop would pop up again during the author's first summer in New York, when his mother and sister stop for a visit. They go see *Black Orpheus*, allegedly the first movie she had seen, at age 16 when she was working as an au pair in Chicago, "the first time that I'd ever been really on my own."

The author explains that, after the movie, without any prompting, "my mother began to retell an old story, in a distant voice, as though she were telling it to herself."

"It wasn't your father's fault that he left, you know. I divorced him. When the two of us got married, your grandparents weren't happy with the idea. But they said okay – they probably couldn't have stopped us anyway, and they eventually came around to the idea that it was the right thing to do. Then Barack's father – your grandfather Hussein – wrote Gramps this long nasty letter saying that he didn't approve of the marriage. He didn't want the Obama blood sullied by a white woman, he said. And then there was a problem with your father's first wife. . . he had told me they were separated, but it was a village wedding, so there was no legal document that could show a divorce. . ."

If Gramps ever said anything about such a letter, it does not emerge in the narrative. The mother seems to realize the problems. Her chin had begun to tremble, the author writes, and she bit down on her lip, steadying herself.

"Your father wrote back, saying he was going ahead with it. Then you were born, and we agreed that the three of us would return to Kenya after he finished his studies. But your grandfather Hussein was still writing to your father, threatening to have his student visa revoked. By this time Toot had become hysterical – she had read about the Mau-Mau rebellion in Kenya few years earlier, which the Western press really played up – and was sure that I would have my head chopped off and you would be taken away.

"When your father graduated from UH he received two scholarship offers. One was to the New School here in New York. The other was to Harvard. The New School agreed to pay for everything, room and board, a job on the campus, enough to support the three of us. Harvard just agreed to pay tuition. But Barack was such a stubborn bastard, he had to go to Harvard. How can I refuse the best education? he told me. That's all he could think about, proving that he was the best."

"We were so young, you know. I was younger than you are now. He was only a few years older than that. Later, when he came to visit us in Hawaii that time, he wanted us to come live with him. But I was still married to Lolo then, and his third wife had just left him, and I just didn't think . . ."

Things are pretty complicated with this group, and in the Kenyan's visit to Hawaii "that time," none of these details came forth. If the Kenyan, married to his third wife and with a large family, had wanted the author's mother Ann to leave Lolo the Indonesian and move to Kenya, that is something any child would be certain to remember. But maybe the mother knows that is all irretrievably lost, because she has more to say.

"Did I ever tell you that he was late for our first date? He told friends 'you see, gentlemen. I told you that she was a fine girl, and that she would wait for me.'"

The author, meanwhile, was finding the career path that was in his genes.

In *Dreams from My Father* the author says, "I decided to become a community organizer." He saw the need for change, particularly in the White House where "Reagan and his minions were carrying on their dirty deeds." The author duly provides more detail on his career choice.

"Becoming an organizer was part of a larger narrative, starting with my father and his father before him, my mother and her parents, my memories of Indonesia with its beggars and farmers and the loss of Lolo to power, on through Ray and Frank, Marcus and Regina; my move to New York and my father's death. I can see that my choices were never truly mine alone – and that is how it should be, that to assert otherwise is to chase after a sorry sort of freedom."

As a scholar such as David Garrow would know, the Kenyan Barack Obama never did anything that could be described as community organizing. Even so, it's all part of the narrative. It wasn't the author's choice, as he explained when his mother told him that his brains and his character came from his father. In *Dreams from My Father*, the author has family in Africa but he never appears to consider living there, even on a short-term basis, say, like those in the Peace Corps. His first choice is Chicago, a city he had first visited "the summer after my father's visit to Hawaii, before my eleventh birthday."

The author had told readers that "during his years in Chicago," Frank had enjoyed some modest notoriety as a contemporary of Richard Wright and Langston Hughes. And Frank was not a forgotten man in the Windy City. In the style of Gramps, the reader might believe it was Frank, not the radical black students, who gave the Hawaiian-born community organizer instant credibility. In these circles, it matters very much who your daddy was. The author is not entirely forgetful.

"I imagined Frank in a baggy suit and wide lapels," he writes, "standing in front of the old Regal Theatre, waiting to see Duke or Ella emerge from a gig." Being a community organizer was "part of the larger narrative" through Frank, among others. The author gets no further contact with Aunt Jane, who called from Nairobi to tell Barry his father had passed away. But one day his sister Auma arrives from Africa, full of information on the Kenyan.

"The Old Man," says the author, "That's what Auma called our father, and it was familiar and distant, an elemental force that isn't fully understood." She held up the picture of their father "that sat on my bookshelf, a studio portrait that my mother had saved." Auma held it to his face and said "you have the same mouth."

As scholarly reviewers and casual readers would note, the studio portrait Auma was holding did not find its way into *Dreams from My Father*. The author is telling readers to accept sister Auma's word that the Kenyan Old Man and his American son have the same mouth. In the style of Gramps, readers who compare the photos might not think so.

At one point the author asks Auma to tell what she remembers about the Old Man.

"I can't say I really knew him, Barack. Maybe nobody did. . . not really. His life was so scattered. People only knew scraps and pieces, even his own children."

Readers would not have to be the erudite David Garrow to note that, unlike aunt Jane, who used "Barry," Auma uses "Barack" for the American and "Old Man" for the Kenyan. If they weren't convinced already, readers might think the Old Man has a real identity problem. Maybe nobody knew him. But Auma reveals a key detail.

"He was already away when I was born. In Hawaii with your mum, and then at Harvard."

So when the Kenyan Barack Obama came to Hawaii, he was already married with a family including Auma. This reality meant that any marriage to Ann Dunham would be invalid, and that posed problems for the prospect of an official divorce. The eager Auma does not trouble herself with the details.

When he came back to Kenya, she explains, "I was too young to remember much about him coming." But he had an American wife named Ruth, "the first white person I had been near."

The Old Man was "working for an American oil company – Shell, I think." And the Old Man was "well connected with all the top government people." In fact, as Auma explains, "the Old Man, he left the American company to work in the government, for the Ministry of Tourism."

These jobs would be a matter of record, especially the government post, and quite a talking point for the man's American-born son, but he appears to have made no effort whatsoever to gather the information. Or maybe he did, and then it was irretrievably lost, like the memories of the month-long visit in Hawaii. In this narrative, he has to get the story hearsay from Auma, who early in the conversion said she didn't really know the Old Man, and maybe nobody did.

As the scholarly David Garrow would note, Auma never describes the Old Man as a pro-Soviet Marxist. In her account, the Kenyan's big issue is tribalism, which he claimed would ruin the country. He always thought he knew best, Auma said, and "When he was passed up for a promotion he complained loudly. 'How can you be my senior,' he would say to one of the ministers, 'and yet I am teaching you how to do your job properly.' Word got back to Kenyatta that the Old Man was a troublemaker."

Thus, Auma, the woman who didn't really know the Old Man, can rattle off quotes of what he said in the workplace, and she knew all about the intrigues in the Kenyan government, headed by strongman Jomo Kenyatta.

Later as she stared at "our father's photograph," Auma laments between sobs, "I was just starting to know him." So when he died, "I felt so cheated. As cheated as you must have felt." But Auma has good news too.

"You know, the Old Man used to talk about you so much! He would show off your picture to everybody and tell us how well you were doing in school."

As the most casual reader would note, Auma doesn't have the picture the Old Man showed off to everybody. But then, she didn't really know him, and maybe nobody did, though she remembers his American wife Ruth the first white person she had been near. He was like a stranger, after all. All told, quite a performance. As Gramps might say, this dramatic narrative requires constant suspension of disbelief.

After the session with Auma, the son says "All my life I had carried a single image of my father." That stands at odds with his earlier statements that he preferred the father's more distant image "an image I could alter on a whim or ignore when convenient." Now it's a single image, "one that I had sometimes rebelled against but had never questioned, one that I had later tried to take as my own. The brilliant scholar, the generous friend, the upstanding leader – my father had been all those things."

The author goes on to tout the black men he knew, "Frank or Ray or Will or Rafiq." The alert reader might note that Frank's name comes first and that the Kenyan Barack Obama, also known as the Old Man, does not even make the list. These men might have fallen short of the standards of "Martin and Malcolm, DuBois and Mandela," but "I had learned to respect these men for the struggles they went through, recognizing them as my own."

As it happens, *Dreams from My Father* contains little about the Rev. Martin Luther King Jr., and that is not accidental. As David Garrow would know, the black American Stalinists hated King and derided him as "De Lawd," the divine character from *The Green Pastures*. American Communists preached Lenin's belief that all worship of a divinity was necrophilia.

Barack, meanwhile, is now in a position to hire people. One employee, Johnnie, asks "Why haven't you ever gone to Kenya?"

"I don't know. Maybe I'm scared of what I'll find out."

Johnnie does not ask the author what, exactly, he might find in Kenya that would scare him. Johnnie helps him work with various churchmen, including the Reverend Jeremiah Wright, Jr., "a dynamic young pastor. His message seemed to appeal to young people like me." The Rev. Wright tells him "life's not safe for a black man in this country, Barack. Never has been. Probably never will be." Yet he titles a sermon "the audacity of hope." In these quarters, Barack ruminates:

"The relationship between black and white, the meaning of escape, would never be quite the same for me as it had been for Frank or for the Old Man." Here the author puts the two men in the same sentence and Frank again takes priority. But in this useful fiction, the Old Man is not about to disappear. Obama Jr. is soon off to Kenya, now evidently unafraid of what he will find there. By the time he makes this trip, the Old Man is dead but his fame lives on.

"You wouldn't be related to Dr. Obama by any chance?" asks Miss Omoro, a woman at the airport.

"Well, yes," he says. "He was my father."

"I'm very sorry about his passing," Miss Omoro says. "Your father was a close friend of my family's. He would often come to our house as a child."

It is an exchange of significance.

"She'd recognized my name," the author says. "That had never happened before. . . for the first time in my life, I felt the comfort, the firmness of identity that a name might provide."

As any reader would note, in Kenya, the author gives "father" a good workout.

"I feel my father's presence as Auma and I walk through the busy street. I see him in the schoolboys who run past us. . . I hear him in the laughter of the pair of university students, . . I smell him in the cigarette smoke of the businessman. . . in the sweat of the day laborer." Indeed, "the Old Man's here, I think, although he doesn't say anything to me. He's here, asking me to understand." Like "father," colonialism is a prevalent theme. The author is asking the reader to understand.

He digs up documents about his Muslim grandfather Onyango including a "passbook," which was characteristic of South Africa, not Kenya. None of the documents is included in *Dreams from My Father*. Back home, Obama gets engaged and takes Michelle to Kenya.

"She was an immediate success there," the author says, "in part because the number of Luo words in her vocabulary very soon surpassed mine."

The audacious, hopeful Rev. Wright marries them, with family in attendance. "The person who made me proudest of all was Roy," the author says. "Actually, now we call him Abongo, his Luo name, for two years ago he decided to reassert his African heritage. He converted to Islam and had sworn off pork and tobacco and alcohol." Roy, his African brother, also pronounces on "the need for the black man to liberate himself from the poisoning influences of European culture, and he scolds aunt Auma for her European ways."

As the scholarly David Garrow would note, this is quite a tale. The author, who has a stubborn desire to protect himself from scrutiny, is out to make a name for himself but not in the usual way through proven accomplishment. Instead he rips off the name from the Kenyan, just as Hannibal Lecter peeled the face off a dead cop in *Silence of the Lambs*. The Kenyan then becomes simply a nameless "Old Man."

The author camouflages the high-profile Stalinist Frank Marshall Davis as Frank, the Grady Wilson-like happy drunk, warning about the dangers of womenfolk. By the time the book emerges, Frank, the Kenyan, Gramps and Ann Dunham are all dead, unable to render reviews, favorable or otherwise. The narrative is also highly didactic, and at pains to create symmetry between British colonialism and America's racist past. But the author tips his hand with the "myth," "tales" and the "useful fiction." He can't honestly say that the voice in the book is not his, a definite tip-off that a ventriloquist is at work, but if people have trouble taking him at face value, he doesn't fault their suspicions. In the style of Gramps, readers might have a hard time finding that "granite slab of truth."

Beyond the confessional aspect, the book is highly contradictory in what it affirms. As prosecutors know, it's harder for someone to keep straight stories that have no basis in fact. As any critic would note, the tale is bulked with evasive filler, the elephantine style blurring the contours like a coating of mud. The fact-checker had an existential problem and the author provides little if any documentation, few dates, no photo section, no photo credits, and squads of characters given first names only, including Frank. So it can hardly be an accident that *Dreams from My Father* fails to include an index. The fakery leapt off the pages, but nobody seemed to notice.

"Perceptive and wise," says the front cover endorsement from Marian Wright Edelman, "this book will tell you something about yourself whether you are black or white."

"Beautifully crafted. . . moving and candid," says novelist Scott Turow on the back cover. "This book belongs on the shelf beside works like James McBride's *The Color of Water* and Gregory Howard Williams's *Life on the Color Line* as a tale of living astride America's racial categories."

"Provocative," wrote the *New York Times Book Review*.

"Persuasively describes the phenomenon of belonging to two different worlds, and thus belonging to neither."

Turning to the other national newspaper of record, the *Washington Post Book World* said, "Fluidly, calmly insightful, Obama guides us straight to the intersection of the most serious questions of identity, class and race."

For Alex Kadowitz author of *There are no Children Here*. "Obama's writing is incisive yet forgiving. This is a book worth savoring."

"One of the most powerful books of self-discovery I've ever read," opined Charlayne Hunter-Gault, author of *In My Place* and PBS correspondent. "It is also beautifully written, skillfully layered, and paced like a novel."

In 2017, Pulitzer Prize-winner David Garrow said it *was* a novel, and the author a composite character. Garrow revealed that fun-loving "Frank" was really Frank Marshall Davis, a Communist, but none of the other critics or investigative journalists proved curious.

Shortly after the book's initial release in 1995, Barack Obama appeared on "Connie Martinson Talks Books" show on public television, which debuted in 1979. Martinson is a member of the National Book Critics Circle and in the early going it was clear she had actually read *Dreams from My Father*. She asked the author why he used pseudonyms but failed to press him on his reason for hiding true identities.

Connie Martinson, who had taught at UCLA, listened in rapture as her guest told the television audience he became a community organizer, "to reestablish the dreams and idealism that brought my parents together." Then she asked him to read from *Dreams from My Father*, which he did. So it wasn't so much an interview as a recital, like something from Oprah Winfrey's show. So was a September 20, 1995 speech the author gave at the Cambridge public library, which aired on Channel 37 Cambridge Municipal Television as part of "The Author Series."

"My father was a black African," he said. "My mother a white American" and "as mid-American as you could get." He is "trying to make sense of my family" and explains that "my father's family came from a small Kenyan village" and his grandfather was one of first to see and have contact with a white person.

The African father and American mother met in Hawaii, "swept up in idealism," and a sense of "community, equity and fairness." But their marriage broke apart. The author reads a passage from the book in which he is angry because his father is absent. He laments that he is "without father figures around me." Then, in this context, he introduces "a black man from Kansas named Frank." He was a "fairly well known poet, moved to Hawaii and lived there." This poet was "Frank Marshall Davis," the speaker said, and "a close friend of my maternal grandfather."

By openly identifying Frank Marshall Davis on a television program, the speaker was handing critics the keys to the mystery, but investigative reporters did not appear eager to follow up. Likewise, the true identities of the pseudonyms and first-name-only characters remained unexplored. In his review of the "historical novel" *Dreams from My Father*, Garrow revealed some key identities, and he took the trouble to familiarize himself with Frank, a photographer with a taste for nudes. Long before *Playboy,* Hugh Hefner and the sexual revolution, Frank had no trouble acquiring subjects.

"I was amazed at the number of gals eager to strip and stand unclothed before the all-seeing eye of the camera. Sometimes husbands brought their wives to pose nude – apparently so that in later years when mates developed middle-aged spread they could look back with graphic nostalgia on what used to be." His friend Thelma, "had no hesitancy about asking a shapely girl to have her picture taken with nothing on her but lights."

As the scholarly Garrow discovered, in 1949 the Communist Party shipped Davis to Hawaii, where the cost of living is high. As John Edgar Tidwell of Miami (Ohio) University explains in his introduction to Davis' memoir *Livin' the Blues*, economic reversals forced Frank to take up the pen "for purely monetary reasons." The result was the 1968 *Sex Rebel: Black*, subtitled *Memoirs of a Gash Gourmet.* Davis used the pseudonym Bob Greene, but clearly it's all about Frank, who owned up to writing it.

"In addition to cunnilingus, at times I enjoy analingus," the author tells readers right up front. "I often wish I had two penises to enjoy simultaneously the sensations of oral and genital copulation." On the other hand, "I realize I would invite trouble if I named those with whom I have enjoyed supreme pleasure." Therefore, says the author, "I have changed names and identities. However, all incidents I have described were taken from actual experiences." And the author gives readers ample reason to believe him.

"I prefer a woman with abundant pubic hair," the black sex rebel explains. "I like the sense of power I feel in bringing a woman to orgasm." Sometime during his Hawaii sojourn, the author met Gwen, whom he dubbed "Gwen the Chick with the Cavernous Cunt" and sometimes "Old Tunnel Twat." Analingus and anal sex with a woman named Dot prompts this meditation:

"It's funny about an asshole," the author writes. "The sphincter muscles are unusually strong and in response it's far tighter than a cunt. Yet it can take a cock just as easily as can a pussy, especially after conditioning. I worked my pole up her educated pit within seconds." And so on, ad nauseam.

In *Sex Rebel: Black* coeds are pining for a good time. In *Livin the Blues*, "summer sessions at the university bring thousands of co-eds intent on having a ball," and "goodly numbers of Caucasian females shed their inhibitions." Hawaii is a paradise with some of the most beautiful women on earth and "Afro-American brothers make out with all kinds of dolls."

The author says that around the age of 55 he began to wonder whether he was still attractive to women. Frank Marshall Davis was 55 in 1960, and an eager coed could be just the ticket he needed to feel good about himself.

"Strange as it may seem," he writes in *Livin' the Blues*, "I have impregnated only three women, all white. One had a miscarriage and the second an abortion." Frank supplies no names for any of the pregnant ladies, but it is certainly possible to guess.

David Garrow noted that Frank wrote to his friend Margaret Borroughs about "my thoroughly erotic autobiography," so in a real sense it was the opposite of the *Dreams* account. That had been a novel disguised as a memoir. *Sex Rebel* was autobiography disguised as a novel.

The scholarly Garrow was also aware that Frank was on the Security Index, a register of the nation's "most dangerous supposed subversives." Frank was also on DETCOM, the FBI's "most wanted" list of top Communists marked for immediate detention in event of national emergency.

In Garrow's account, when Davis first sees young Barry he says

"Oh, this is him?" Garrow does not comment on the remarkable physical similarities but says only that "Barack would forcefully reject the Davis hypothesis." Still, Garrow states that "Davis' Communist background plus his kinky exploits made him politically radioactive."

"My father was an African American, born and raised in Kansas, and college educated. He loved jazz, wrote poetry and made a name for himself in Chicago. A prolific journalist interested in politics, he chose to join the Communist Party, dominated by whites. He spent most of his life as a propagandist for the Soviet Union, ruled by an all-white dictatorship. They made some mistakes but, more important, they wanted a better world. My father wanted a better world, and so do I."

Such an introduction would have suited the man the author lovingly described as "Pop," but even the Democratic Party is unlikely to welcome Pop with open arms. A politician on the rise needs something more along these lines:

"My father was a foreign student, born and raised in a small village in Kenya. He grew up herding goats, went to school in a tin-roof shack. His father, my grandfather, was a cook, a domestic servant to the British."

That was candidate Barack Obama in his keynote address to the Democratic Party convention on July, 27, 2004. The 2004 edition of *Dreams from My Father* included the entire speech and that year the author won his race for U.S. Senator from Illinois, defeating Alan Keyes, also an African American, by a wide margin. In 2005, an audio version of the *Dreams* book appeared with a significant omission: every single mention of Frank had been removed. So the author's stubborn desire to protect himself remained strong. In politics, as the Kennedy and Bush families know, it does matter who your daddy was.

That year the U.S. Senator for Illinois won a Grammy for the audio version, bagging the prize for best spoken word over Garrison Keillor's *The Adventures of Guy Noir: Radio Private Eye*, *The Al Franken Show Party*, Bob Dylan's *Chronicles: Volume One*, and *When Will Jesus Bring the Pork Chops?* by George Carlin. But the rising star did not rest on his laurels. With his new identity, and the uncritical reception of *Dreams from My Father*, the possibilities seemed endless.

The Audacity of Hope: Thoughts on Reclaiming the American Dream appeared in 2006 and readers could see the difference right up front. The Hawaiian-born American calling himself Barack Obama is on the cover, which shows no thatched huts or any African motif.

Still, people ask, "where'd you get that funny name?" On page 10, he explains:

"I am a prisoner of my own biography: I can't help but view the American experience through the lens of a black man of mixed heritage, forever mindful of how generations of people who looked like me were subjugated and stigmatized, and the subtle and not so subtle ways that race and class continue to shape our lives."

A scholarly author and critic such as David Garrow would note the "prisoner of my own biography" story of the African father from Kenya and the American mother from Kansas. That's the story in *Dreams from My Father* and the author realizes there's no escape from it. On the other hand, the Kenyan Old Man plays little role in *The Audacity of Hope*, where the mother is the prime mover.

"Much of what I absorbed from the sixties was filtered through my mother, who to the end of her life would proudly proclaim herself an unreconstructed liberal. The civil rights movement in particular inspired her reverence; whenever the opportunity presented itself, she would drill into me the values that she saw there: tolerance, equality, standing up for the disadvantaged." His mother, "worked mightily to instill in me the values that many Americans learn in Sunday school; honesty, empathy, discipline, delayed gratification, and hard work. She raged at poverty and injustice and scorned those who were indifferent to both."

She did this without the help of religious texts or outside authorities, but she did teach him about religion. This differs from the account in *Dreams from My Father*, in which she refuses to describe her faith as religious and even finds it "sacrilegious." And she was a "lonely witness for secular humanism." *The Audacity of Hope*, on the other hand, transforms Ann Dunham into a one-woman ecumenical movement.

"In her mind," the author says, "a working knowledge of the world's great religions was a necessary part of any well-rounded education. In our household, the Bible, the Koran, and the Bhagavad Gita sat on the shelf alongside books of Greek and Norse and African mythology." The author does not single out any one as particularly influential, as he did the autobiography of Malcolm X in *Dreams from My Father*.

The *Audacity of Hope* does not recall Malik, the Nation of Islam convert who explained that Malcolm X "tells it like it is, no doubt about it." The author is not a theologian but here he seems to show a flair for political philosophy.

He quotes the Declaration of Independence and traces its roots to eighteenth-century liberal and republican thought. The value of individual freedom, he writes, was "as radical as Martin Luther's posting on the church door." Much of humanity finds scant evidence of freedom in their lives.

"In fact," the author explains, "my appreciation of the Bill of Rights comes from having spent part of my childhood in Indonesia and from still having family in Kenya, countries where individual rights are almost entirely subject to the self-restraint of army generals or the whims of corrupt bureaucrats."

As the scholarly David Garrow would know, that fit Indonesia more than Kenya, for all its difficulties one of the more democratic countries in Africa. Even as a British colony, freedom, democracy and human rights thrived more in Kenya than Tanzania and Mozambique, whose flag bears the image of a Russian AK-47 rifle. As in *Dreams*, those regimes escape notice here.

The author says he took Michelle to Kenya shortly before they were married and "we had a wonderful time, visiting my grandmother up-country." Where, exactly "up-country" might be on the map is not noted but the folksy formulation seems to indicate long familiarity with the nation of Kenya. On the flight back to Chicago Michelle says "I never realized just how American I was."

If the author experiences any feelings like Michelle's he keeps them to himself. In *Dreams from My Father*, his role models are his Kenyan father and grandfather. In *The Audacity of Hope* he draws lessons from Illinois Senator Paul Simon, admiring his honesty, character, and sense of empathy. And "like most of my values, I learned about empathy from my mother. She disdained any kind of cruelty or thoughtlessness or abuse of power." He also mentions another source.

"But it was my relationship with my grandfather that I think I first internalized the full meaning of empathy," and this is not the Kenyan Hussein II Onyango, who worked as a servant to the British. The author is talking about Gramps, Stanley Dunham, the white American from the Kansas heartland. "I often lived with my grandparents during my high school years, and without a father present in the house, my grandfather bore the brunt of much of my adolescent rebellion." As for the Kenyan:

"My father was almost entirely absent from my childhood, having been divorced from my mother when I was two years told." But the reader gets some insights on the man.

"Although my father had been raised a Muslim, by the time he met my mother he was a confirmed atheist, thinking religion to be so much superstition, like the mumbo-jumbo of witch doctors that he had witnessed in the Kenyan villages of his youth."

A scholarly critic or general reader might recall that the Kenyan had explained all that during the month-long visit, and it was all coming back to the author now. So it wasn't irretrievably lost after all.

The book downplays the Kenyan Barack Obama, and the *Audacity of Hope* title, readers learn, comes from a sermon by the Rev. Jeremiah Wright, whose anti-American fulminations, "god damn America," that sort of thing, get no coverage here. The book is packed with policy wonkery and populist pieties, wrapped in flag-waving patriotism all the way to the last line:

"My heart is filled with love for this country."

The critics loved it.

The author was "that rare politician who can actually write," wrote Michiko Kakutani in the *New York Times*, citing the book's "simple common sense," and "level-headed non-partisan prose."

John Balzer of the *Los Angeles Times* praised the author's "fresh and buoyant vocabulary to scrub away some of the toxins from contemporary political debate."

For Michael Kazin of the *Washington Post*, the book's "uplifting, elegant prose does fill one with hope."

Like *Dreams from My Father,* this book lacks a photo section and the index has no entry for anyone named Davis. At the Cambridge Library in 1995, the author identified "Frank," as Frank Marshall Davis and in the *Dreams* book Frank gets first place on the author's list of influential black men in his life. More than a decade later, in *The Audacity of Hope*, Frank is missing altogether, just as he was from the audio version of *Dreams from My Father*. On the other hand, as Garrow and other scholarly critics might note, a key character missing from that book duly shows up in this one.

David Axelrod makes several appearances in *The Audacity of Hope* as a "media consultant," with little background information. In the acknowledgements section, Axelrod heads the list of "good friends" who provided invaluable suggestions.

On April 1, 2007, Ben Wallace-Wells profiled David Axelrod in a *New York Times* article headlined, "Obama's Narrator." In this article of more than 5,000 words, Obama's narrator tells Wallace-Wells that Obama is a "trailblazing" figure who "represents the future." Gramps might get the distinct feeling that David Axelrod is really behind this guy.

Wallace-Wells does note that Axelrod was a former lead political reporter for the *Chicago Tribune* but left that post to work as a political operative. In 1987 *Chicago Magazine* profiled him in "Hatchet Man: The Rise of David Axelrod." Wallace-Wells notes that in the last four years, "Axelrod has helped steer campaigns for fully four of the Democrats now running for president – Obama, Clinton, John Edwards and Chris Dodd."

So the author of *Dreams from My Father* and *The Audacity of Hope* has good reason to thank the man profiled as "Obama's narrator," who tells reporters that his candidate represents the future itself. The author also thanks Madhuri Kommareddi, who devoted the entire summer before she entered Yale Law School, to "fact-check the entire manuscript" with help from Hillary Schrenell. By all indications, over an entire summer this team found no issues of fact with the biography of which the author was a prisoner. So the fact checkers found true that the Kenyan Barack Obama, though "raised a Muslim" as the author explains, was an atheist who dismissed religion "like the mumbo-jumbo of witch doctors that he had witnessed in the Kenyan villages of his youth."

The checkers did not have to chase down all the facts on Frank because Frank wasn't in the book. As Gramps might say, out of sight, out of mind. And as far as the checkers are concerned, the narrative of the African father and American mother is part of a body of unassailable fact. As it happens, fact-checker Madhuri Kommareddi went on to work as a policy aide on the Obama for American 2008 presidential campaign.

During that campaign, as Barry Rubin noted in *Silent Revolution: How the Left Rose to Political Power and Cultural Dominance,* influential writers, academics and members of the press on the confidential

JournoList spoke of how to be most effective in ensuring Obama's election victory in 2008. Yet, says Rubin, "not a single serious investigation was conducted about Obama's earlier life." That remained shrouded in secrecy or decked out in disguise as in *Dreams from My Father*. Voters knew less about the man calling himself Barack Obama than any candidate in U.S. history.

"We are five days away from fundamentally transforming the United States of America," proclaimed the candidate on October 30, 2008, in Columbia Missouri.

As Rubin noted, FDR's New Deal and Lyndon Johnson's Great Society had already transformed the nation into a top-heavy welfare state. So voters might wonder what the candidate was talking about, and why details of his early life were in such short supply.

With Frank, the Kenyan Old Man, Gramps and Ann Dunham all dead, Madelyn Dunham, the candidate's maternal grandmother, was the person most in the know. Reporters were not eager to seek her out, but she wasn't in the habit of talking to them. Madelyn Dunham passed away at 86 on November 3, 2008, one day before her grandson became president of the United States, the most powerful man in the world. His early life remained mysterious but in due course the nation would learn about his mother.

The definitive treatment of Obama's mother, Ann Dunham, comes from *New York Times* reporter Janny Scott, whose *A Singular Woman: The Untold Story of Barack Obama's Mother* from Riverhead Books appeared in 2011, the same year as Sally Jacobs' *The Other Barack*. Scott's book has no index and the epigraph is from the preface to the 2004 edition of *Dreams from My Father*:

"I think sometimes that had I known she would not survive her illness, I might have written a different book – less a meditation on the absent parent, more a celebration of the one who was the single constant in my life."

As *Dreams from My Father* makes clear, she was not the single constant in his life, far from it. The epigraph to the preface is also of interest.

"I am the son of a black man from Kenya and a white woman from Kansas," Barack Obama, March 18, 2008.

With an introduction like that, readers are unlikely to find any challenge to the president's official story. Scott is aware of the controversies but instead of probing the issues the *New York Times* reporter opts for quick and glib dismissal:

"And in the fevered imaginings of supermarket tabloids and the Internet," Scott writes, "she is the atheist, the Marxist, the flower child, the mother who 'abandoned' her son or duped the state of Hawaii into issuing a birth certificate for her Kenyan-born baby on the off chance that he might want to be president someday." Scott in effect adds to the controversy, and the title of her book is already misleading.

Anyone writing about Ann Dunham, Scott explains, must address the question of what to call her. She was Stanley Ann Dunham at birth and Stanley as a child. She dropped Stanley after high school. Then came Ann Dunham, then Ann Obama then Ann Soetoro until her second divorce. She modified that name to Sutoro and in the early 80s she was Ann Sutoro, Ann Dunham Sutoro and S. Ann Dunham Sutoro on her dissertation. So she wasn't exactly a "singular" woman, and Scott opts to call her "whatever name she was using at the time." Among those, "Obama" is definitely outnumbered.

Scott's main source is "President Obama's sweet and lyrical *Dreams from My Father*, woven from tales he was told as a child." Unlike David Garrow, Scott did not find the book to be a novel rather than a memoir, but she did find a few errors. Obama writes that his mother was born at Fort Leavenworth, the Army base where Stanley was stationed. But Scott learns that Ralph Dunham, Stanley's older brother, said he visited mother Madelyn and her baby in Wichita Hospital when the child was a day or two old. So it wasn't Fort Leavenworth. And mother Ann would later say, "she had nearly entered the world in a speeding taxi." The author does not note when she said this, nor to whom.

Scott gives some background on Hawaii and the East-West Center the U.S. federal government established there "to exchange ideas, information and beliefs through cooperative study," with advisers including UN undersecretary Ralph J. Bunche.

Maya, Ann's daughter with the Indonesian Lolo Soetoro, told Scott, "We often would say that Mom met her husband at the East-West Center," while conceding, Scott adds, "that it was not strictly true." The Kenyan student Barack Obama was not on an East-West Center grant and in fact the center had not yet been built. So what they would say was in fact false, "but the family myth contained a kind of truth," the *New York Times* reporter explains. "Wherever Ann and Obama met, it was in a moment suffused with the spirit in which the center was born."

Scholarly critics and casual readers alike might wonder about "a kind of truth." Could a witness in a murder trial swear to tell "a kind of truth," for example? Would the author undergo an operation by someone whose claim to a medical degree was "not strictly true"? And since Maya's admission comes from an actual family member, readers might wonder if other accounts of how the couple met were "not strictly true" or possibly just suffused with "a kind of truth."

One friend, whom Scott does not name, "said he remembered Ann saying she met Obama in the library," but according to the younger Obama, "they met in a Russian language class." Scott leaves it to the reader to decide which account in the family myth is true, or a kind of truth.

The Kenyan Barack Obama arrives one month after Hawaii's statehood, with 80 other Kenyans, sponsored by Kenyan nationalist Tom Mboya. Obama is "charismatic and sharp" and to Americans "his accent suggested Oxbridge, and his booming baritone voice brought to mind Paul Robeson."

As critics would be quick to note, the Robeson comparison is not a direct quote from anybody Scott interviewed. In the sweet, lyrical *Dreams from My Father*, neither Ann Dunham nor the author describe the Kenyan's voice as a booming baritone that brought to mind Paul Robeson. For his part, the *Dreams* author can't remember a single thing the Kenyan said during an entire month, but he does remember that Frank was a comrade of Paul Robeson. As it happens, Frank Marshall Davis, though less talented, did have a deep voice like Robeson's.

Scott cites accounts from graduate students such as Pake Zane, Chet Gorman and Neil Abercrombie. Also cited is Richard Hook who worked with Obama years later in Kenya. By all accounts he was smart and charismatic, a straight-A student, who commanded attention when he spoke. None describe the Kenyan as a fan of American jazz, Dave Brubeck, or rock and roll, which *Dreams from My Father* takes such pains to establish. And as Scott says "not everyone was charmed" by the man.

Some found Obama arrogant, egotistical and overbearing. White Kenyan Mark Wimbish found him domineering, a man who could not abide the views of others. Judy Ware, a Dunham friend, recalled meeting Obama "sometime later in Port Angeles, Washington," a remote place the Kenyan never shows up in the sweet and lyrical *Dreams from My Father*. Neither does he show up there in *The Other Barack* or any newspaper accounts. Scott provides no date for the encounter but Ware describes Obama as "outgoing, friendly, and that he was flirtatious, and that made me uncomfortable. He was just a bit intimidating to me. He was too close in my personal space" and "I thought he was a little bit almost aggressive in his way of meeting and being around women."

In Scott's account, the couple meet in the fall of 1960. She is seventeen and he is twenty-four. "Though he apparently omitted to mention it initially," Scott writes, "Obama was a married man, with a wife and child in Kenya and a second child on the way."

Ann had never had a boyfriend and was a virgin, according to Kadi Warner, Ann's graduate school friend. "Some years later" Ann told Warner she was "totally enthralled" by Obama, who was brilliant, striking and exotic. According to Warner, he courted her and she was attracted to him. Said Warner, "I doubt he was the sort of man who would have carried a condom in his pocket" and "many years later" Warner said Ann married Obama because she was pregnant.

As with many a subject, the Kenyan's own views on birth control are not on record. Interestingly enough, as David Garrow might have noted, in *Sex Rebel: Black*, Frank Marshall Davis makes clear his disdain for condoms. And he is certainly flirtatious and aggressive with women, very close in their personal space. As he said in *Livin' the Blues*, "summer sessions at the university bring thousands of co-eds intent on having a ball." And as the couple from Seattle told him, "quite a few coeds are available for special affairs."

Scott cites *Dreams from My Father* about the meeting in Russian language class and falling in love. The Kenyan's charm wins over the parents and he marries the girl, who bears him a son "to whom he bequeathed his name." He leaves for Harvard without money to take his family, then returns to Africa. The mother and child stay behind but the bond of love survives the distances.

Scott notes that Obama wrote his account when he was in his early thirties, "at a time when his mother and grandmother were alive and well, and available for consultation." But Obama, "offers little in the way of alternative version" and "It appears that parts of the account he was told were wrong."

Ann gets pregnant, drops out of school and marries Obama discreetly, but there's no record of a real wedding, a cake, a ring, a giving away of the bride. No families were in attendance, and people back in Kansas were not informed.

In Scott's account, on 7:24 p.m. on August 4, 1961 at Kapit'olani Maternity and Gynecological Hospital in Honolulu, Ann gives birth to Barack Hussein Obama Jr. So the identity of the father and the bequeathing of his name was not the part of the account that Obama got wrong. At no point does Janny Scott, *New York Times* reporter, challenge what she calls the "family myth," a term that also appears in the sweet, lyrical *Dreams from My Father*, which also talks of a "useful fiction." Eleven months later, meanwhile, "the elder Obama was gone."

Scott then turns to the *Honolulu Star-Bulletin* article Obama Jr. said he found along with his birth certificate and vaccination forms, while in high school. This article said the elder Obama had departed to tour mainland universities before entering Harvard. The article does not mention the child or his mother.

In her notes section, Janny Scott says this piece came from the *Honolulu Star-Bulletin*, June 20, 1962, which is correct. She is also correct that it was four paragraphs long and ran on page 7. Scott does not directly quote the piece but explains that the Kenyan had been awarded a graduate fellowship in economic planning and planned to return later to Africa to work in economic development and international trade planning and policy.

In *Dreams from My Father* Obama's narrator says that the piece had a photograph of the Kenyan. Scott does not mention the photo and it does not appear in *A Singular Woman*. Neither does a photo of the birth certificate and vaccination records Obama Jr. says he found along with the article. Putting that in the book would have been an easy way to quiet those fevered imaginations of supermarket tabloids and the Internet. On the other hand, Scott's book does have photos scattered through the text, and they too are of interest.

None has a credit on the page on which the photo appears. The book has no table of contents but tucked away at the back readers find notes on the photo sources. These come from Ann's classmates, colleagues, field assistants, a driver, and professors. Some came from Ann herself and others came from "family members and friends of Ann Dunham, some of whom chose not to be credited by name." The author offers no reason why they should decline to be identified.

"Some of the images in this book," Scott concedes, "were made public during the 2008 presidential campaign by Obama for America, the campaign organization." These include the black-and-white photo on page 144 of Ann "With Barack Obama Sr. Christmas 1971," as the line below explains. The smiling Kenyan, in a suit and tie, has his left arm around Ann, with his hand resting on her shoulder. It is the only photo in the book of Ann and the Kenyan together.

Also from the Obama for America campaign is the black-and-white photograph on page 145 showing "Barack Obama Sr. and the young Barack, Christmas 1971." The Kenyan has his left arm around the young Barack, who has his arms folded over the Kenyan's hand. Two of the Kenyan's fingers protrude from below, and seem out of proportion to the size of the hand. Young Barack is looking at the camera, but the Kenyan is not. Both photos are rather blurry, particularly the background, which appears to be an airport terminal. A sign in the upper left reads San Francisco. Both photos have a crude, cut-and-paste look that stands in stark contrast to the photos from other sources, none of which show the Kenyan and Ann together.

The other photos from Obama for America show "Stanley and Barack" at the beach and Ann "with Lolo, Maya, and Barack, 1970." Readers get no information on any of the photo sources until the final two pages of the book. The omissions are also significant.

In *Dreams from My Father*, the author describes a photo of himself holding the orange basketball he says his Kenyan father gave him, and a photo of the Kenyan with the tie that the lad gave him. These photos (page 70), taken "in front of the Christmas tree" were "the only ones I have of us together." *Dreams from My Father* and *The Audacity of Hope* did not include that photo, and neither does *A Singular Woman*. So the pictures may have an existential problem.

As Scott tells it, Ann left Hawaii before Obama Sr. did. Ann's friend Maxine Box saw her in Seattle in the summer of 1961, all happy and proud of her baby but, "saying nothing about marriage." Indeed, "Her sudden motherhood startled friends" and the news of Ann's pregnancy, sudden marriage and separation was "closely held" within the Dunham and Payne families. Ralph Dunham, Ann's uncle, did not get the news of the pregnancy and marriage until after the child was born.

Ann enrolled at the University of Washington for the spring quarter of 1962 and after the semester returned to Honolulu. She divorced Obama in 1964 and on March 5, 1964, married Lolo Soetoro. Janny Scott tracks some difficulties with that union.

"The status of Ann's marriage was ambiguous, it seems. According to Obama's account, Ann had separated from Lolo. But that was less clear to friends." According to Kadi Warner, who like Ann had secured a grant from the East-West Center, "she certainly considered herself married."

Janny Scott evidently failed to ask any of Ann's friends about the poet Frank, who gets a full 2,500 words in the sweet, lyrical *Dreams from My Father.* In *A Singular Woman* Frank gets zero words, though some accounts of the Kenyan do seem more like Frank. All told, the mysteries of fatherhood remain but Scott does shed some light on Ann's life, which shows no interest in Russian language, Kenya, the Kenyan Barack Obama, or Africa in general.

In a letter to Bill Byers, "the wheelman on the fateful Cadillac-convertible flight to the San Francisco Bay Area," Ann tells Bill she got the East-West grant, and when that's gone:

"I shall be most content to spend the rest of my life in obscure corners of the world. Probably a useless sort of life, and not very socially relevant, especially since I hate applied anthropology (neo-colonialism in bad disguise – I had a lot of bad experience with it in Asia.) I do hope to spend most of my time for the next few years in the islands since my son Barry is doing very well in school there, and I hate to take him abroad again till he graduates, which won't be for another six years."

So despite the Kenyan "bequeathing" his name, and Miss Hefty's grade-school proclamation that "Barack is such a beautiful name," his mother Ann still calls him Barry, and so do friends such as Kadi Warner. Ann may have considered her life useless but Janny Scott provides more detail on the American woman from Kansas than the sweet, lyrical *Dreams from My Father* does on the Kenyan.

Sally Jacobs 2011 book focused on the "other" Barack Obama but also proved enlightening on Ann Dunham and the parental issues. For example, in 1997, the Barack Obama of Chicago disavows any claim on the Kenyan's estate, worth about $57,000 at the time he died. A claim on the Kenyan's estate, a scholarly critic might note, could elicit legal challenges the *Dreams* author might not welcome. So he backed off.

When the Kenyan was studying at the University of Hawaii in the fall of 1960, Jacobs writes, he enrolled in a Russian language class taught by Ella Wiswell in Room 209 of the new Physical Science building. One of his classmates was "a slender young woman with expressive brown eyes." That is Jacobs' description, not Ella Wiswell, who is not quoted. The Russian-born University of Hawaii professor died in 2005 at the age of 96.

For her part, Ann was shy, but "had asserted herself as an iconoclast, and independent thinker with decidedly liberal views. Like many self-respecting teenagers she abhorred the deadly conformity of the suburbs. She was an atheist who sported a campaign button for Democratic presidential candidate Adlai Stevenson and liked foreign movies and jazz. . . A dreamer like her father, she had a tendency to romanticize that enabled her to glide over human failings and foibles."

In Jacobs' account Ann is "exceptionally bright," and with a "vast vocabulary and intellect to match, she could hold her own on most any subject. And she didn't hesitate to challenge the sacred cows of her era. What was so good about democracy? What was so bad about communism? And why was capitalism so great?"

This doesn't sound much like the *Dreams from My Father* account of the "awkward, shy American girl" who fell for the brilliant African student in Russian class at the University of Hawaii. On other hand, these are not quotes from Ann Dunham and the author does not cite any of Ann's friends in this connection. Stanley Dunham, a military veteran, does not exactly bring to mind a "dreamer."

Jacobs does note that Ann's father would not let her enroll at the University of Chicago or the University of Washington "as many of her friends intended to do." Dunham and her parents headed for Honolulu a few days after commencement and, "Dunham was angry at her father, with whom she already had a prickly relationship." Ann quickly adapted to Hawaii and was soon wearing shorts and muumuus to class, and "dating an African from Kenya." In Jacobs' account "he called her Anna and their courtship was as swift as it was intense" and her primary source is *Dreams from My Father*. Ann called her new love "the African," prompting friends to ask if he had a name.

"Obama, however, said nothing of his new girlfriend to most of his friends on campus," writes Jacobs. In *Dreams from My Father*, on the other hand, he talked her up big time, telling friends "I told you she was a fine girl." Soon Anna the fine American girl was pregnant but the iconoclastic challenger of sacred cows like democracy had no problem with the bourgeois institution of marriage, and that to a man already married, with children. In Jacobs' account that took place on February 2, 1961, in Wailuku, a quiet civil ceremony with neither family in attendance, no cake and no ring, the description from *Dreams from My Father*. According to friends Jacobs interviewed, Ann broadcast the news that she had married the African, was now Mrs. Barack Obama, and "we are expecting a baby in the summer." The Kenyan's response was rather different.

"As usual he told none of his friends that he had gotten married or was expecting a baby." Jacobs also finds evidence in an INS memo that Ann made efforts to give up the baby for adoption. Nothing along those lines appears in *Dreams from My Father*.

"It is possible, the *Boston Globe* journalist writes, "that Obama Sr., not always beholden to the truth, simply lied about the matter." She does not explore the possibility that there was no wedding, that the baby was not the Kenyan's, and that the President of the United States and his handlers "simply lied" at any point.

The author of *Dreams from My Father* is candid that much of what he told about the Kenyan Old Man was "a lie," part of the useful fiction. And the Kenyan Old Man was a prop in someone else's narrative, a character who could be altered at will or ignored when convenient. Jacobs does not explore these questions but she did find that the Salvation Army, where Dunham allegedly made efforts to give up the baby, "declined to discuss the matter, citing privacy regulations."

Robert Gibbs, White House press secretary, told Jacobs that the president never heard that either of his parents considered putting him up for adoption and that the president had not seen the INS memo. The president himself also declined to be interviewed on the subject, still showing that stubborn desire to protect himself from scrutiny. Jacobs mentions the Certification of Live Birth "issued by the State Health Department and publicly released by Obama's presidential campaign" but *The Other Barack* does not include a photo of the document. Neither did *Dreams from My Father* or *The Audacity of Hope*.

In the fall of 1961, only months after the birth, Ann Dunham moved back to Seattle and enrolled at the University of Washington. As Janny Scott noted, she told her friends nothing about a marriage. Jacobs cites no sources that place the Kenyan in Port Angeles, Washington, where he appears in Scott's book. In *The Other Barack*, the Kenyan is back east, describing his family as a wife and two children in Kenya, and making no mention of Ann Dunham and Barack Obama Jr. to college admission officials. *The Other Barack* includes no photo of the Kenyan and Ann Dunham together. The book does include the photo of the Kenyan and his son, from the Obama 2008 presidential campaign captioned:

"The two Barack Obamas pose for a photo that was apparently taken in Honolulu in 1971. The Christmas visit was the only time the two were together after the elder Obama left his small family in Hawaii to attend Harvard University in 1962."

Jacobs does not comment on the photo's rough cut-and-paste look, but it was "apparently" taken in 1971. In *Dreams from My Father*, which Jacobs quotes uncritically, the author recalls not a single statement from that Christmas 1971 visit. The *Boston Globe* reporter does not speculate how it could all be "irretrievably lost." On the other hand, she is willing to concede that the Kenyan had a casual relationship with the truth and might have "simply lied." She does not hint that the author of *Dreams from My Father* might have "simply lied" about anything. With reporters and biographers alike, this man can do no wrong.

In *Rising Star*, official biographer David Garrow noted the "Pop" poem but the Pulitzer Prize winner ignored a milestone book on the man the *Dreams* author had publicly named as Frank Marshall Davis.

In 2012, as the presidential election approached, Paul Kengor, professor of political science at Grove City College, published *The Communist: Frank Marshall Davis: The Untold Story of Barack Obama's Mentor*. This thoroughly researched 400-page work charted how Frank kept busy in Chicago with journalism and worked with a number of CPUSA front groups. Then in 1948 the Party packed him off to Hawaii, where Frank wrote for the *Honolulu Record*, a publication backed by the CPUSA and the International Longshoremen's and Warehousemen's Union, headed by Harry Bridges, another Communist and Soviet agent. *The Communist* details Davis' journalism there, the same pro-Soviet boilerplate he produced in Chicago. He blasted opponents as fascists, racists, Ku Kluckers, Nazi storm troopers and so on. His primary political targets were Democrats, particularly U.S. President Harry Truman. As *The Communist* notes, Frank Marshall Davis' FBI file runs 600 pages, longer than Kengor's book, *Dreams from My Father,* and *The Audacity of Hope.*

Frank Marshall Davis, Communist Party card number 47544, was a supporter of the Soviet Union. His white Party bosses were always right and the Stalinist Davis was a crusader for "the triumph of Soviet power in the United States," as his Party oath stated. This was "Frank," the man to whom the author of *Dreams from My Father* had devoted 2,500 words, but who had disappeared in the audio version and made no appearance at all in a 10,000-word *Washington Post* article on Obama in Hawaii by presidential biographer David Maraniss. Journalists and liberal biographers, Kengor wrote, showed "unscholarly bias" and were "dutifully doing backflips to protect Barack Obama." As Gramps might say, they showed a stubborn desire to protect the president from scrutiny.

For his part, Paul Kengor noted "remarkable similarities" between the columns of Frank Marshall Davis and the political actions and views of President Obama. Frank marched in May Day parades, and so did Obama as a U.S. Senator. Frank hated the British in general and Winston Churchill in particular. President Obama, removed a bust of Churchill from the Oval Office and returned it to the Brits. Frank advocated government wealth redistribution, and so does the president because, as he contends, the free market doesn't work and has never worked.

Frank bashed Wall Street, and so does the president. Frank was not a believer in American exceptionalism and neither is the president, whose narrative creates a symmetry between America's past and colonialism. Frank attacked big business, bankers and big oil, and targeted corporate executives for not paying their fair share. He hated the

"GOP" tax cuts he said only benefitted millionaires. And Frank was fond of slogans such as "change" and "forward." As Kengor noted, "the list goes on and on," and his book is also informative on Chicago's old Stalinist network, from which key presidential advisors David Axelrod and Valerie Jarrett emerged. As Kengor saw it, "the ghosts of Chicago's frightening political past are alive and well in Washington today." His book detailed Communist Party influence on the Democratic Party, so no surprise that the old-line establishment media did not welcome *The Communist* with open arms and open minds. Scholarly author David Garrow ignored the book, no surprise given its treatment of the "Davis hypothesis," which the president "forcefully" rejected.

In *The Communist,* Kengor discussed the president's "Pop" poem, which is clearly about Davis, a poet. The author of *Dreams from My Father* never uses Pop for the Kenyan, whom he calls the Old Man. Kengor speculates that "Pop" might be a simple term of endearment for Frank in the style of Pittsburgh Pirates slugger Willie Stargell, whom fans called "Pops" late in his career. A better example would have been "Sanford and Son," the popular 1970s television comedy, in which son Lamont always used "Pop" for his father Fred Sanford. And when an old friend of Fred's claims to be Lamont's real father, Lamont proclaims Fred "the only Pop I've ever known."

Even so, professor Kengor makes it clear he is not prepared to argue that Frank Marshall Davis is the president's biological father. That was the contention of a documentary also released in 2012, and ignored by official biographer David Garrow.

Joel Gilbert's *Dreams from My Real Father* details the back story of the Stalinist left in Chicago where Davis was a big star. All the White House players are in there, including red diaper baby David Axelrod, Obama's narrator, who signs off on his every word, according to the *New York Times*. The documentary is also thorough on its central theme.

Stanley Dunham is working for the U.S. government and keeping tabs on Frank at a time when the Soviet Union has designs on Hawaii. Stan's daughter Ann, short of friends, duly shows up in Frank's photo studio and gives him the benefit of hindsight and foresight. Viewers can see the photos Frank took and the magazines in which they appeared. Viewers don't see Ann giving Frank the kind of access he described in *Sex Rebel*, but Frank didn't like condoms and, as the gypsy woman said, she soon had a boy child coming. The film gets into that whole dodge with the Kenyan student who supposedly "bequeathed" his name to the child, along with his career. In *Dreams from My Father*, the author's mother told him his career choice to be a community organizer was "all in the genes." *Dreams from My Real Father* raises questions about whose genes were in play.

In the comparison photos, as Auma might say, the president and Frank do indeed have the same mouth. Frank looks more like the president than the Kenyan, and the physical resemblance could explain the dearth of photos and documents in *Dreams from My Father*, and the effort to tell readers what the Kenyan looked like. In reality, Gramps might say the president looks an awful lot like Franky Davis Jr.

Gilbert's film contends that the president even got a nose job to throw people off the scent. The older the president gets, the more he looks like Davis. In fact, he looks as much like Frank Davis as Arnold Schwarzenegger looks like Joseph Baena, the child he fathered with his housekeeper. And in film footage, the old Stalinist sounds a lot like the 44th president.

As journalist Mark Tapson noted in a review of Gilbert's documentary, "the 'birthers' have been on a fool's errand. To understand Obama's plans for America, the question is not 'Where's the birth certificate,' but 'Who's the real father?'" This matters, Gilbert said in an interview, because "promoting a false family background to hide an agenda irreconcilable with American values is a totally unacceptable manipulation of the electorate."

The president's handlers attacked the film, and as Gilbert told this writer, "they went out of their way to condemn me, while never denying that Davis was Obama's father, nor addressing the premise of the film." But Gilbert got some confirmation in a different way. In September of 2012, he received an email from Obama's deputy campaign manager Julianna Smoot offering voters a chance to win a dinner with the president.

"You can learn a lot," Smoot wrote. "His dad taught him to love jazz. . ."

Gilbert was familiar with the president's official story line, that he was with the Kenyan only a single time in the early 1970s, and that he remembered not a single statement or exchange from the entire encounter. The biggest jazz aficionado in the president's life was Frank Marshall Davis, who writes about jazz at length in *Livin' the Blues*. In Chicago, the author of *Dreams from My Father* writes, "I imagined Frank in a baggy suit and wide lapels, standing in front of the old Regal Theatre, waiting to see Duke or Ella emerge from a gig." He also wrote in the "Pop" poem that "I see my face within Pop's black-framed glasses." Yet as far as Gilbert knew, nobody had ever directly asked the president about the man who so resembled him, physically and politically. And as the scholarly David Garrow explained, the author of the *Dreams from My Father* novel, rejected the "Davis hypothesis."

For his part, Joel Gilbert duly tracked down Malik Obama, the Kenyan's oldest son, who found "a great resemblance," telling the filmmaker, "I think Frank Marshall Davis and Barack, they look alike. Some kind of moles I see on his face and Frank, he has those too. There's a resemblance." Malik Obama was even willing to conduct a DNA test.

"That would really prove whether we are related or not," Malik said. "Yes. I would be willing to do that. I don't know how I'd deal with it, if it really came out that he really is a fraud or a con." No DNA test took place, but late in his second term, "Obama's narrator" would provide evidence to back up Malik Obama's question.

In 2015, the president's close advisor David Axelrod released *Believer: My Forty Years in Politics*, a memoir of his own from Penguin Press a division of Random House, which published *Dreams from My Father* and *The Audacity of Hope*. As it happens, the massive *Believer* is about David Axelrod his own self.

In the "Roots" section the author notes that his father, Joseph Axelrod, came to America from Eastern Europe, fleeing violence targeting Jews. Who was doing the targeting is not exactly clear. In America, Joseph Axelrod listed his political party as Communist, and this became an issue when he was due for promotion in the military. So "Communist," which showed up so early in *Dreams from My Father,* appears again here, in upper case. Axelrod does not explain why his father, who like Frank came up during the Stalin Era, might have been attracted to this murderous totalitarian movement.

Joseph Axelrod pursued a doctorate in psychology and his wife Myril, David's mother, wrote for *PM,* the New York daily funded by

Marshall Field, which had a "decidedly leftist bent" and where "progressive literati" thrived. Of them was novelist Howard Fast, who in 1956, after Khrushchev's revelations about Stalin, left the Communist party and wrote *The Naked God: The Writer and the Communist Party*. Fast denounced Communism as an ideology of terror and ignorance, and praised America as a land that defended the rights of the individual.

Axelrod's mother eventually left journalism and became vice president of Young and Rubicam, one of nation's largest advertising agencies. Says the author, "I credit much of my professional success to the drive and skills I drew from her." He would use those skills in Chicago, the city of the big shoulders, as he calls it. Axelrod got a job with the *Hyde Park Herald* where he met David Canter, son of Harry Canter, another Stalinist and secretary of the Communist Party in Boston and a Communist Party candidate for governor in Massachusetts.

As Paul Kengor notes in *The Communist*, Harry took his entire family to the USSR in 1932, the year Stalin's forced famine in Ukraine claimed millions of lives, and the *New York Times'* Walter Duranty denied that any famine took place. Canter left the USSR in 1937, when Stalin's purges and repression still raged. Harry's son David attended the University of Chicago and wrote for the student newspaper. He also edited *Champion*, the newsletter of the Packinghouse Workers Union, subject of activism by Frank Marshall Davis and Vernon Jarrett. The Canter family was also familiar with Frank as a writer for the *Chicago Star*, whose contributors included I.F. Stone. David Canter set up Translation World Publishers, which published Soviet propaganda.

Believer includes nothing on Harry Canter, David Canter, Vernon Jarrett, Robert Taylor, and Frank Marshall Davis, all part of the Stalinist network in the city with the big shoulders. In the early 1970s, that network was still working three shifts for the Soviet Union. Frank was legend in those circles but he's missing in action here, just as he conveniently disappeared from the audio version of *Dreams from My Father* and developed an existential problem in *The Audacity of Hope*. *Believer* has an index but it includes no entry for Frank or for *Rules for Radicals* author Saul Alinsky another *capo* of Chicago's old left and a mentor to many left-wing candidates, including Hillary Clinton. The book and its index also exclude the Kenyan foreign student Sally

Jacobs profiled as *The Other Barack,* the "old man" from *Dreams from My Father* who bequeathed his name to an American child. Axelrod conveniently makes the African disappear, just as Stalin ordered Leon Trotsky airbrushed out of official photographs.

Axelrod moved on to the *Chicago Tribune* but like his mother he left journalism and began working for politicians, becoming communications director for Illinois Senator Paul Simon. "I was surprised at how easy it had been," Axelrod wrote, "to trade in those tools for a new career, and how naturally I'd adjusted to my new role."

Axelrod believes that "authenticity is an indispensable requirement for any successful candidate, but particularly for a president. Biography is foundational. More and more, I had become convinced that voters were inured to slick, highly produced media, and the antidote was this more genuine, documentary-style approach. Part of that might have been defensive, since I felt more comfortable, and proficient at, telling stories than I did creating the ads that were state-of-the-art in Washington."

The comfortable, proficient storyteller would soon have a candidate more to his liking than the jug-eared, bow-tied liberal Paul Simon, who wanted a balanced budget. He worked with Hillary Clinton, another Saul Alinsky disciple, but she was not the one.

At one point, "I got a perfectly timed and unexpected call from an old friend that would change my life." As the believer writes:

"David, it's Barack," said the voice on the phone. "I'm thinking about what I want to do next, and was wondering if we could talk." The language is significant.

In *Dreams from My Father*, the Kenyan and his mother called the shots: "I would follow his example, my mother decided. I had no choice. It was all in the genes." The author also wrote: "I can see that my choices were never truly mine alone – and that is how it should be, that to assert otherwise is to chase after a sorry sort of freedom." In Axelrod's account, he is a mature, independent man who makes his own decisions and thinks about what he wants to do next.

David Axelrod says he met Barack Obama in 1992 a year of significance that could explain the reference to perfect timing.

On February 8, 1992, Stanley Dunham passed away at the age of 73. So Gramps was no longer around to offer insights on family history, correct any written accounts that might appear, or perhaps write one of his own. Believer David Axelrod makes no reference to Stanley Dunham.

On the timing side, 1992 was the first full year after the demise of the USSR, which left Communists with lost hopes. That same year the University of Wisconsin Press released Frank Marshall Davis' *Livin' the Blues: Memoirs of a Black Journalist and Poet.* For Axelrod and his eager client, the appearance of this book was a mixed bag.

The introduction by John Edgar Tidwell of Miami University acknowledges that Frank Marshall Davis is the author of *Sex Rebel: Black* subtitled, *Memoirs of a Gash Gourmet*. Frank himself owned up to the novel and even at a Democratic Party convention in San Francisco anyone associated with the book might not get a warm welcome. But *Sex Rebel: Black* was not the only problem.

In *Livin' the Blues* Frank Marshall Davis was totally candid about being a Communist and made it clear that he joined the CPUSA after the Hitler-Stalin Pact, when many others, black and white, left for good. So Frank's goose-stepping Stalinism was not the ticket for a warm reception, even in Democratic Party circles, but the problems did not end there.

Livin' the Blues included photos of Frank Marshall Davis, and the ones on pages 308 and 310 show remarkable resemblance to the American calling himself Barack Obama.

"I knew Barack was an exceptional writer," Axelrod contends, without explaining how he knew it. The president never authored news stories, feature articles, reviews and such. He has not made available any senior thesis from his college days, and he produced not a single signed law review article. If he was in fact an exceptional writer, why the need to approach proficient storyteller David Axelrod?

"What animated *The Audacity of Hope,"* Axelrod explains, "were stories written with the narrative skill of a gifted novelist." The self-described comfortable and proficient storyteller thinks the author of *The Audacity of Hope* is *really good.*

"It occurred to me, in reading the manuscript," Axelrod writes, "that Obama approached every encounter as a participant and an observer. He processed the world around him with a writer's eye, sizing up the characters and the plot, filing them away even as he fully engaged in the scene. He has an appreciation for irony and a firm grasp on the fact that some things remain beyond our control. It's a quality that contrib utes to his outward calm, even amid utter chaos."

Axelrod was writing three years after Paul Kengor's *The Communist: Frank Marshall Davis: The Untold Story of Barack Obama's Mentor*, and three years after Joel Gilbert's *Dreams from My Real Father* documentary. Both contained considerable material on Frank Marshall Davis and his Chicago colleagues Vernon Jarrett and Robert Taylor. Both mention President Obama's close adviser David Axelrod and *The Communist* devotes attention to President Obama's close adviser Valerie Jarrett, granddaughter of Vernon Jarrett and Robert Taylor, and their connections to Frank Marshall Davis. *Dreams from My Real Father* is very thorough on Chicago's Stalinist network, and viewers get to see and hear Frank his own self.

In *The Communist*, Paul Kengor wrote that pro-Soviet propagandist David Canter mentored David Axelrod, but Axelrod's massive work of more than 500 pages contains nothing on Kengor's book and Gilbert's documentary. Axelrod also ignores the birth controversy, even those "birthers" who focused on the location of the president's birth, not the identity of the father. The believer who is proficient and comfortable telling stories won't touch any of that, just as the president himself declined to discuss Sally Jacobs' question about his mother considering adoption.

Believer would have been the best opportunity for Obama's narrator, who sat closer to the Oval Office than anybody else, to slap down the birthers by providing the documentation they sought. He's not up to that task, and does not reveal any of the material the president took a lot of trouble to block, his academic records, admission forms and such. On the other hand, he does equate opposition to the president with racism.

Criticism of Obamacare, for example, was not due to anyone losing the health plan they liked, contrary to what they had been told. It was not due to a dysfunctional website, billions in waste, security risks, or anything like that. Nor was it the imposition of this system with no meaningful debate.

For the believer David Axelrod, criticism of Obamacare "was rooted in race: a deep-seated resentment of the idea of the black man with the Muslim name in the White House. The facts notwithstanding, to them, health reform was just another giveaway to poor black people at their expense." Just kind of a simple thing, but more to come.

"Some folks," says the believer, "simply refuse to accept the legitimacy of the first black president and are seriously discomforted by the growing diversity of our country."

Everything in Axelrod's 2015 *Believer* would have been of great interest to official biographer David Garrow, winner of a Pulitzer Prize. "Obama's narrator," as Axelrod was known, sat near the president and signed off on virtually everything he said. Even so, Garrow does not mention Axelrod until page 820 of *Rising Star*, and does not take up themes such as Axelrod's story-telling prowess and the timing of the *Dreams* book, the "useful fiction" that Garrow proclaimed a novel in 2017.

"A WHOLE DIFFERENT TYPE OF MOTHERFUCKER"

With a rising star like the former Barry Soetoro, audiences could have expected a movie treatment in the early going, say, around 2004, when Barry delivered the big lines about his Kenyan father, or perhaps during his brief sojourn in the U.S. Senate. Nothing of any consequence appeared until 2016, when *Newsweek's* Matthew Cooper noted: "There's less than a month left of Barack Obama's presidency but the 55-year-old remains enigmatic. His remarkable ascent—as the son of a mixed-race marriage, the child of a single mother in Hawaii—to the Oval Office is as great a Log Cabin tale, as that of any of his 43 predecessors. Maybe it's because of his swift rise or his outlier/insider duality that he remains, even in his last days in office, the object of so much dispute."

As Cooper notes, "the president has already penned two deservedly acclaimed memoirs and more are planned," but the writer mentions none of the material in those books that might have left the president "enigmatic" and the subject of "dispute." The president is now "the subject of two biopics, this summer's charming *Southside with You*, about his first date with Michelle Robinson, "and now *Barry*, a Netflix production that charts his college years in New York, when 'Barry,' as he was known, wrestled with his racial identity."

As Cooper explained, "I was at Columbia a year behind Obama," who transferred from Occidental College in 1981 but "I never knew Obama." As Cooper recalls, Clinton factotum George Stephanopoulos was a year ahead of Barry and didn't know him either. Neither did many other Columbia students, including those in Barry's class.

"I don't know a single person at Columbia that knows him, and they all know me. I don't have a classmate who *ever knew* Barack Obama at

Columbia. Ever!" That was Columbia alum and Libertarian Party vice presidential candidate Wayne Allyn Root in 2008.

As Root told Matt Welch of *Reason* magazine, he and Obama were in the same class: "Class of '83 political science, pre-law Columbia University. You don't get more exact than that. Never met him in my life, don't know anyone who ever met him. At the class reunion, our 20th reunion five years ago, 20th reunion, who was asked to be the speaker of the class? Me. No one ever *heard* of Barack! Who was he, and five years ago, nobody even knew who he was." And the person who wrote up the class notes for the reunion, "who knows everybody, has yet to find a person, a human who ever met him. Is that not strange? It's very strange." Root also thought it odd that the student he never saw, reportedly very smart, "won't release his transcripts from Columbia University."

In 2013, Root wrote in *Human Events* that at Columbia University the president "was Pre-Law and a Political Science major – just like me. I thought I knew everyone studying Political Science during my four years at Columbia. Not Obama. I never met him, never saw him, never even heard of him. Strange. Same major, same career path, and graduated on the same day. Where was he?" So Root raises the possibility that the president is "a fraud."

In 2010, Brooks Jackson of FactCheck.org, a publication of the Annenberg Public Policy Center, addressed Root's doubts. Jackson cited Columbia's claim that Obama was a graduate, a profile of him from 2005, and an article the student wrote in the *Sundial*, a Columbia publication. On the other hand, Jackson found only a single student, Phil Boerner, who said he roomed with Barry during his time at Columbia and remembered much of anything about him. As it happened, Wayne Allyn Root, Matthew Cooper and George Stephanopoulos are hardly the only Columbia students with no memories of Barry.

"We were his classmates in the Columbia University undergraduate class of 1983," wrote Judy Maltz in a March 15, 2013 article in the Israeli publication *Haaretz*. Maltz numbered close to 25 in the group of 1983 Columbia grads including lawyers, one doctor, several engineers, an architect, librarian, speech pathologist, financier and a journalist. The group also included two married couples who began dating at Columbia.

"But here's the thing," Maltz explained. "Not one of us remembers Barack Obama – who transferred to Columbia after his sophomore year at Occidental College in California – from our undergrad years, nor do we know anyone else who does."

Jamie Miller, a mother of five active in the Columbia alumni association, travels back to New York every five years to attend reunions. "I was in the marching band, I worked on the yearbook, and I was involved in student government, so I knew everyone," explained the librarian and English teacher. "But I never saw him around."

Speech pathologist Sarah Graber Nehrer was living in Illinois when the former Barry Soetoro ran for the Senate. She had gone to school with the Columbia alum, "but I had no recollection of him whatsoever, and neither did anyone else I know, which I found very strange."

Wayne Sohn, an inventor of medical devices, said he didn't take pride in having gone to Columbia with the president, "But sure, if he's willing to meet us, I'd be happy to go." As Maltz noted in 2013, "the group of Columbia 1983 alumni has submitted a request with the U.S. Embassy in Tel Aviv to meet with their former classmate, but have yet to receive a response."

The president of the United States, the most powerful person in the world, was not willing to meet with such an accomplished group of Columbia grads. Like Wayne Allyn Root, they found that very strange. As viewers might expect, none of this mystery shows up in *Barry*, which dramatizes the period that has touched off so much dispute.

In Cooper's review, Barry (Devon Terrell) "arrives in New York smart and quick, a standout in his classes, ridiculously handsome, exotic and athletic to boot." But despite his intellect and gifts, "Barry doesn't fit in. He's singled out for questioning by a campus cop and ridiculed by the locals in his Harlem neighborhood. And as one "ghetto-raised" student says "You a whole different type of motherfucker, B."

Critic A.A. Dowd found that "*Barry* plucks an anecdote about *Black Orpheus* from the president's best-selling memoir, *Dreams From My Father: A Story Of Race And Inheritance*."

For Dowd, Obama himself potentially deserves story credit, "given how much psychology, insight, and incident the film draws from his autobiography. Certainly, the book inspired some of the nested daddy issues," which Dowd fails to probe.

For Manola Dargis of the *New York Times*, "it's all a bit much too much, this white girl buying this particular black guy a Baldwin book." But every so often, Dargis wrote, "Barry takes out a letter from his father."

Dargis failed to note that in 2013, the Harlem-based Schomburg Center for Research in Black Culture invited the president to review the Kenyan Barack Obama's written communications from 1958-1964, including more than 20 letters. In all these writings the Kenyan mentions nothing about an American wife and Hawaiian-born son. So no surprise that the president never showed up, just as he showed no inclination to meet with fellow Columbia graduates.

The people who saw no trace of Barry at Columbia, and didn't know anybody who did, outnumber those who did see him, and their accounts are more convincing. The prospect that the president might have been a fraud, as Root said, failed to pique the interest of investigative journalists in the establishment media. Like the tame journalists covering FDR, they simply looked the other way and wrote nothing.

By all indications, the Netflix production *Barry* is simply a cinematic treatment of the *Dreams* book and its "useful fiction." Viewers might note that in 2018, POTUS 44 and his First Lady signed a multi-year deal with Netflix, as *Variety* noted, to "work on scripted and unscripted series as well as docu-series, documentary films, and features." More sequels to *Barry* are doubtless in the works.

Meanwhile, in the summer of 2016, A.A. Dowd wrote, "*Southside With You* dramatized Barack's first date with Michelle, spinning the events of a single day in August 1989 into a speculative Chicago romance featuring two colleagues blissfully unaware that they'll eventually be the first couple." In addition, "in its sweetly featherweight manner, is a more resonant work: It simultaneously depends less on the legacy of its subject *and* gets closer to capturing his dignity, his intelligence, his appeal as a public figure."

Neither film mounts any challenge to the official story. In 2017, official biographer David Garrow, a winner of the Pulitzer Prize, would explain why the author of *Dreams from My Father* remained enigmatic and a matter of dispute.

After more than 1,000 pages, Garrow cites Gabriel Sherman of *The New Republic* that "reporters who have covered Obama's biography or his problems with certain voter blocs have been challenged the most aggressively." And an unidentified reporter makes this statement about the president's staff:

"They're terrified of people poking around Obama's life. The whole Obama narrative is built around this narrative that Obama and David Axelrod built, and, like all stories, it's not entirely true. So they have to be protective of the crown jewels."

That is the narrative of *Dreams from My Father*, and on page 538 of *Rising Star: The Making of Barack Obama*, Pulitzer Prize winner David Garrow says the *Dreams* book "was not a memoir or an autobiography; it was instead, in multitudinous ways, without any question *a work of historical fiction*" and the author a "composite character."

The scholarly Garrow notes the author's beloved Frank but "Davis' Communist background plus his kinky exploits made him politically radioactive." Nobody is going anywhere in American politics by touting a Stalinist pornographer. So in 1992, after Gramps passed away, the author got on the phone with David Axelrod and the storyteller came up with a new narrative. A brilliant African student named Barack Obama fell in love with his mother and "bequeathed his name" to the American.

"How Stanley Ann Dunham's relationship with Barack Obama commenced and developed," Garrow explains, "remains deeply shrouded in long unasked and now-unanswerable questions." Trouble is, the Harlem-based Schomburg Center for Research in Black Culture houses the Kenyan Barack Obama's written communications from 1958-1964, including more than 20 letters. In all these writings the Kenyan mentions nothing about an American wife and Hawaiian-born son. In 2013 the Center invited the President of the United States to come and have a look his own self. As with the Israeli Columbia students, he never showed up.

Those realities managed to escape the scholarly Garrow, who does cite the reporter that the narrative Obama and Axelrod built is "not entirely true." So the scholarly Pulitzer Prize winner helpfully left the key by the back door.

Trouble was, the composite character of the *Dreams from My Father* novel, whose story was "not entirely true," had been president of the United States for the past eight years. Wayne Allyn Root, who like many others never saw the president when he claimed to be at Columbia, finds similarities with the plan of former Columbia professors Cloward and Piven who "taught that America could only be destroyed from within." This would be accomplished by "overwhelming the system with debt, welfare, and entitlements," so the plan was "to make a majority of Americans dependent on welfare, food stamps, disability, unemployment, and entitlements of all kinds. Then, under the weight of the debt, the system would implode and the economy collapse, bankrupting business owners (i.e. conservative donors). Americans would be brought to their knees, begging for big government to save them." In 2013, Root saw this unfolding "right in front of our eyes."

Under Obama, Root observed, "660,000 Americans dropped off the job rolls… *just last month*. 90 million working-age, able-bodied Americans are no longer in the workforce. *90 million.* The workforce participation rate is the lowest since 1979. For men it's the lowest since 1948. (when record keeping began). Almost 50 million Americans are on food stamps (20 percent of all eligible adults). 14 million are on disability. Millions more are on welfare, unemployment, housing allowances, aid to dependent children, or 100 other free government programs. Now, add in free healthcare plus 22 million government employees. Record-setting numbers of Americans are emptying their retirement accounts to survive. Student loan debt is a national disaster – with defaults up 36 percent from a year ago. 16.4 million Americans live in poverty *in the suburbs*. Every day under Obama the private sector shrinks, while the government grows like a toxic malignant tumor."

Obama promised to cut the deficit in half but "instead he gave us five consecutive trillion-dollar deficits. He promised to spend responsibly; instead he became the biggest spender in world history. He called Bush's $4 trillion in debt over eight years reckless, then proceed to pile on $6 trillion in only four years. He swore to be on the side of small business, but he added 6,118 new rules, regulations and mandates in just the last *90 days*. He claimed taxes are low, yet he just raised taxes to the same level as bankrupt EU countries like Greece, Spain, Italy and France. Our federal income taxes are now far higher than former Soviet Republics."

For the libertarian Root, "this is no accident, or the work of an economically inept liberal." And "this is no coincidence. This is the

Marxist attack from within. This is a purposeful attempt to take down the economy, collapse the middle class, wipe out small business, bankrupt the wealthy (conservative donors), and addict the country to big government Nanny State socialism." The president achieved considerable success along those lines, but it wound up working against him.

The composite character also did his best to transform the nation into a more autocratic arrangement in which the outgoing president picks his successor and does everything in his power to ensure her election. Despite considerable effort involving intelligence and law enforcement agencies, the nation rejected former First Lady and Secretary of State Hillary Clinton. That left the composite character's echo chamber and publicity agency – the old-line establishment media – utterly bewildered and deranged, and they were in no mood, as one reporter told Garrow, to "poke around" in the composite character's life. Likewise, few general readers, even those favorably disposed to the composite character, were eager to crack open a book of more than 1,000 pages that weighed in at five pounds.

For their part, the nation's critical class had been in on the *trahison des clercs* from the start. Some members pronounced that *Dreams from My Father* was a groundbreaking memoir that read like a novel. Few if any critics were now eager to read a book that said the *Dreams* account *was* indeed a novel, and the author a composite character.

In 2017, after eight years of the composite character as the most powerful man in the world, few if any critics were eager to learn of the erudite girlfriend Genevieve Cook who started, and ended, her poem to Barry with, "You masquerade, you pompous jive, you act."

Few if any critics were eager to track down the reporter who told David Garrow that the president's staff is "terrified of people poking around Obama's life. The whole Obama narrative is built around this narrative that Obama and David Axelrod built, and, like all stories, it's not entirely true. So they have to be protective of the crown jewels."

The critics, who long ago junked their bullshit detectors, were terrified of anything that might challenge the narrative. The *soi disant* "presidential historians" who hold forth on PBS were not curious about Frank Marshall Davis, even after the scholarly Garrow noted that the kinky pornographer and pro-Soviet Communist was on the security index, and therefore "politically radioactive" for young

Barry. He needed a different narrative, and in 1992, after Gramps conveniently died, the Hawaiian-born American tapped his storyteller pal David Axelrod to put it all together. Even after the erudite David Garrow had confirmed the narrative as fiction, without any question, the faithful were terrified and rushing to the barricades to protect the crown jewels.

After eight years of his boss in the White House, nobody was panting for book by Deputy National Security Advisor Ben Rhodes, a chief promoter of the Iran deal. Still, in 2018, a year after *Rising Star*, Ben Rhodes came out with *The World As It Is: A Memoir of the Obama White House.* Rhodes explains he reported to David Axelrod, "a brilliant strategist who weighed in on every issue." According to Rhodes, the president's "first memoir, *Dreams from My Father*, is a kind of Rosetta Stone to Obama's life and world view." Rhodes claims he reread it "a dozen times," and in all those readings apparently noted none of the difficulties and contradictions that jump off the page, including the author's boast of a "useful fiction." Rhodes, who aspired to be a novelist, never notes that official biographer David Garrow pronounced the book without question an historical novel and the author a composite character. Readers of *The World As It Is* get no clue that *Rising Star: The Making of Barack Obama* even exists.

For the creative Rhodes, Obama was "a symbol for the aspirations of billions of people" and questions about his story amounted to "outright racism." That was the defense mechanism the president's narrator David Axelrod had outlined in *Believer*, entirely predictable, fully understandable, and completely without significance. The former Deputy National Security Advisor had not noticed that the Kenyan Barack Obama, in all his writings from 1958 to 1964, mentioned nothing about an American wife and Hawaiian-born son.

Rhodes had not sounded out the Israeli students who had been at Columbia University the same time as his boss, yet had no memory of him and knew nobody who did. Rhodes never ran that by high-profile Clinton mouthpiece George Stephanopoulos, who was a year ahead of Barry at Columbia but never knew him, nor the journalist Matthew Cooper, who was a year behind Barry but never knew the future president.

The former Deputy National Security Advisor took no notice of

Paul Kengor's *The Communist: Frank Marshall Davis: The Untold Story of Barack Obama's Mentor*. That marked a contrast from David Garrow, who noted that Davis was a Soviet agent and on the FBI's security index. Rhodes may have re-read the *Dreams* memoir a dozen times, but never wondered why "Frank," disappeared from the audio version and made no appearance at all in *The Audacity of Hope*.

Ben Rhodes likewise ignored Joel Gilbert's *Dreams from My Real Father*, very thorough on "Frank," and his startling physical resemblance to Rhodes' former boss. And Rhodes failed to trace the "birther" charge to members of Hillary Clinton's 2008 campaign.

Rhodes showed no curiosity about Barry's trip to Pakistan as a student, and why that had failed to emerge during campaigns. The White House security advisor did not recall his former boss telling Dimitry Medvedev that Vladimir Putin needed to be patient, and that he would have more flexibility after the election.

On the other hand, the White House insider pays tribute to "brilliant strategist David Axelrod," who "weighed in on every issue." True to form, *The World As It Is: A Memoir of the Obama White House,* by aspiring novelist Ben Rhodes, is pure damage control, a coverup, and retroactive hagiography.

Also in 2018, Michelle Obama put out her memoir *Becoming*. The former First Lady recalled the "birther" claim that her husband wasn't born in the United States and called it "crazy and mean-spirited." It was "deliberately meant to stir up the wingnuts and kooks" and posed a danger to the family, particularly the daughters. Like her husband's founding narrative, that is not entirely true.

Dreams from My Father did not launch a flurry of inquires whether the author had been born in Kenya. Nobody raised questions about the author's authenticity until 2004, when political gadfly Andy Martin charged that the *Dreams* author was a Muslim who concealed his religion. That was picked up by columnist Debbie Schlussel in 2006 and in 2007 Clinton strategist Mark Penn proposed an attack on Obama for his lack of American roots.

The charge that Obama had been born in Kenya first appeared in April, 2008, when supporters of Hillary Clinton circulated an anonymous e-mail questioning Obama's citizenship. If true, it disqualified him to run for president, clearing the way for Clinton to be the Democrat candidate. That didn't happen in 2008, but the birther claim served as a convenient diversion from inquiries about the identity of Barry's father. Michelle Obama isn't about to go there, and she does her best to shore up the *Dreams* narrative.

Michelle's husband, the future president, "sold his idea for a nonfiction book about race and identity." For obvious reasons, she doesn't mention that in the 2017 David Garrow proclaimed the alleged "nonfiction book" a novel and the author a composite character.

She married an "out-of-the-box thinker" who "steered himself with a certainty I found astounding." On the other hand, he had influences such as Valerie Jarrett, deputy chief of staff to Chicago mayor Harold Washington.

"Valerie was the right person to address any concerns," Michelle writes. "Valerie was like a fast-moving comet and clearly going places." Jarrett went on to wield great power in the White House, a defacto first lady on policy issues.

Valerie spent her childhood in Iran, "where her father had been a doctor at a hospital." Michelle does not divulge that Valerie's father, James Bowman, and her father-in-law Vernon Jarrett were both Communists and associates of Frank Marshall Davis, the beloved "Frank" of *Dreams from My Father*. Frank does not appear in *Becoming*, so the racially conscious Michelle missed an opportunity to explain the devotion of a black American to all-white Communist dictatorships. As the Columbia students said of her husband's absence at the Ivy League school, that is strange, very strange.

About halfway through *Becoming*, readers meet David Axelrod, who would "lead the messaging and media for Barack." True to form, Axelrod's fingerprints are all over this account, and in his 2015 *Believer*, Axelrod explains that he left journalism because he liked to tell stories. He described Obama, who had no record of publication, as a fantastic writer with the skill of an historical novelist.

Michelle writes that her husband "spent the first 20 years of his life going by the nickname Barry," but "somewhere along the way, though, he'd stepped into the fullness of his birth name—Barack Hussein Obama." He just stepped into it, and as *Dreams* had it, the name had been "bequeathed" to him. The former First Lady thus ignores the *Dreams* account, in which the author claims that that the

Kenyan used "Barry" as a nickname, even though many characters, including the Kenyan, call the author "Barry." So no surprise that the former First Lady ignores David Garrow, whose massive *Rising Star* calls the *Dreams* book fiction and the author a composite character. But like Garrow, Michelle fails to note that the Kenyan Barack Obama, in all his writings from 1958 to 1964, mentioned nothing – not a single word – about an American wife and Hawaiian-born son.

As the Hawaiian-born American said in his "useful fiction," *Dreams from My Father*, the Kenyan Barack Obama was a "prop," that the author "could alter on a whim or ignore when convenient." Still, as he said, people had a hard time taking him at face value, so he maintains that "stubborn desire to protect myself from scrutiny."

In *Becoming*, Michelle is protecting her husband from scrutiny. At that task, he would enjoy more help than any fake in history.

"I first came to Chicago when I was in my early 20s, still trying to figure out who I was," the 44th president said in January of 2017. In reality, he already knew who he was, and why he came to Chicago. That was where the beloved "Pop," Frank Marshall Davis, made a name for himself. That connection gave him instant credibility with Frank's old network, but as David Garrow noted, "Davis' Communist background plus his kinky exploits made him politically radioactive." To get anywhere in American politics, he would need a new identity and a new back story.

The Hawaiian-born Barry Soetoro could have simply adopted an African or Arabic name in the style of Stokely Carmichael, who took the name Kwame Toure, or H. Rap Brown who became known as Jamil Abdullah Al-Amin. Instead Barry would claim to be the actual son of the Kenyan Barack Obama, the brilliant African student at the University of Hawaii who supposedly "bequeathed" his name to him. In 1992, after his grandfather Stan died, the storyteller David Axelrod helped Barry cobble together *Dreams from My Father*. As the senatorial candidate told the Democratic Party convention in 2004:

"My father was a foreign student, born and raised in a small village in Kenya. He grew up herding goats, went to school in a tin-roof shack. His father, my grandfather, was a cook, a domestic servant to the British."

As Michael Corleone said in *The Godfather*, that's a terrific story. The old-line establishment media liked the story so much they accepted it uncritically, and attacked anybody who didn't. Four years later the composite character became president of the United States, the most powerful man in the world.

In the early going as president, the man who linked his career to his Kenyan father showed little interest in Africa in general and Kenya in particular. Readers of *Dreams from My Father* might have expected the president to announce a Marshall Plan for the continent, with special attention to Kenya, that victim of British colonialism. The president did no such thing and made only one trip to Kenya, in July of 2015, when he joked about looking for his Kenyan birth certificate. In the early going of his first term, he did not seek any advisers from that nation, perhaps a relative, a colleague, or even one of the Kenyan's college professors.

On the other hand, on the foreign policy front, he gave Russia essentially everything Kremlin bosses wanted, in 2009 cancelling missile defense for U.S. allies Poland and the Czech Republic. And in 2012 he told Russian president Dimitry Medvedev he would have "more flexibility" to deal with contentious issues such as missile defense after the election.

It was like Auric Goldfinger, after his Fort Knox attack failed, making a last stand in the uniform of an American soldier. And like Olympic officials in 1972, who stole the victory of the American men's basketball team, the African-American president put time back on the clock for Cuba's Communist regime, headed by white Sado-Stalinist Fidel Castro. The beloved Frank, so fond of all-white Communist dictatorships, would have approved, but there was more to it.

The American president, raised in Indonesia, was also an asset for Muslim regimes, proclaiming that the future must not belong to those who slander the prophet of Islam. On the way out the door, he shipped billions in cash to the Iranian mullahs, still chanting "death to America," fueling terrorism, and working three shifts on a nuclear weapon.

At the end of *The Audacity of Hope*, the composite character candidate proclaimed "My heart is filled with love for this country." As composite-character president, it was more like "your country, right or wrong."

As narrator David Axelrod explained in *Believer*, the president's "longer game" was to transform the United States, already a welfare state from the days of FDR's New Deal and LBJ's Great Society. As the late political scientist Barry Rubin noted in *Silent Revolution*, the president enjoyed great success at selling the idea that the statist, high-regulation policies that had failed so spectacularly in Europe were precisely what America needed.

The old-line establishment media helped seal the deal, and Republicans, for all their talk of free enterprise, offered only token opposition. If you have a business, the president said, you didn't build that. It was all Big Brother's idea. So it follows that, in the America of the composite-character president, you don't get what you want. You get only what the government wants you to have.

If you like your health plan, you could keep it, the composite character said. Trouble was, you couldn't. It was the greatest "taking" in U.S. history. Like his eponymous health care plan, you had to elect the composite character to find out what he was about.

The composite character also surpassed other presidents in deploying the IRS and DOJ against his domestic opposition. And not a smidgeon of corruption was involved, the most powerful man in the world said.

On November 5, 2009, at Fort Hood, Texas, self-proclaimed "Soldier of Allah" Maj. Nidal Hasan yelled "*Allahu akbar*" gunned down 13 unarmed American soldiers, including Pvt. Francheska Velez, 21, who was pregnant, and wounding more than 30 others. The president of the United States did not call this terrorism or even "gun violence." The president of the United States called it "workplace violence," as though the homicidal soldier of Allah had been a disgruntled postal worker. Those who thought that absurdity was the low point in his presidency were wrong. Much worse was to come.

The commander in chief of U.S. armed forces deployed the upper reaches of the DOJ, FBI and intelligence communities to ensure that his chosen successor Hillary Clinton, whom he touted as more qualified than any person in history, became president of the United States. When she lost, the president deployed his deep state forces to discredit the victor, and change the result of the election by toppling him from office.

As John Goodman said in *The Big Lebowski*. "This is what happens, Larry, when you fuck a stranger in the ass." In similar style, the disastrous record of 2008-2016 is what happens when you elect as president of the United States a composite character whose memoir is a novel, and whose dreams come from the Communist Frank Marshall Davis. The composite character's greatest success was passing himself off as something he was not, and that made the steady demolition possible. Nothing quite like that ever happened before, and the dynamics of the age were on his side.

The composite character and his narrator telegraphed the fakeries with a flare gun. Never had an obvious composite character been greeted with such willful blindness and fathomless credulity, with considerable lend-lease from the establishment media. As with the crippled FDR, they formed a tight circle around the president, lest anybody see him take a fall.

By the time of the composite character's appearance, the eschaton had been thoroughly immanentized. In these conditions, a narrative that needed factual verification instead demanded uncritical *belief*, so no accident that the composite character's narrator David Axelrod titled his own memoir *Believer*.

Gutless politicians duly fell in line, fearing to raise any questions, lest the believer call them racists. Others more in line with his politics drew inspiration from the composite character's politics drew inspiration. Identity politics also played role.

In this belief system, it is someone's "turn" to be president based on factors he or she can't control, such as skin color or gender. The election of such a person on that basis is held to be a marker of progress and social justice, regardless of performance.

Elizabeth Warren claimed to be Cherokee, but she wasn't. At this writing, Harvard's first "woman of color" is still contending for the White House, telling anybody who will listen that if they have a business, they didn't build that. After the success of the composite character, a fake can keep on campaigning even after their fakery is exposed.

Kevin de Leon, whose name on his birth certificate and voter rolls is Kevin Alexander Leon, claimed his father was a Chinese cook from Guatemala. He wanted to be the Latinobama, uniting Asians and Hispanics as the composite character claimed to unify blacks and those people of no color. Nobody in the establishment media bothered to investigate his obviously bogus story. At this writing the man "known professionally" as Kevin de Leon is running for the city council of Los Angeles.

Sen. Richard Blumenthal claimed he was a Vietnam veteran, seeking to climb the political ladder on the backs of those who were. He was hoping that nobody in the establishment media would check but somebody did. No Vietnam veteran smacked him upside the head, as he so richly deserved. Nobody demanded that he resign, and he didn't.

Harvey Milk claimed the U.S. Navy kicked him out for being homosexual. That wasn't true, and neither was the claim that Milk was the victim of an anti-gay bigot. Even so, Milk got a U.S. Navy ship named after him and an airport exhibit hailing the un-outed pederast as a heroic "Messenger of Hope."

Congressional candidate Ammar Campa-Najjar claimed to be the son of a Hispanic woman from the barrio and an Arab man from an occupied territory. The father wanted America and America wanted him, and he met his mother in sunny San Diego before returning to the "occupied territory." He didn't mention that his grandfather was one of the 1972 Munich terrorists, and when that emerged he pretended to condemn it before expressing doubts. He lost in 2018, but now runs again as a Hispanic Arab-American and Palestinian Mexican without any calls for documentation from the establishment media. Like the president he worked for, the Latino Arab American is also a composite character in a fictional narrative.

This is what happens when you immanentize the eschaton. This is what happens when pretenders and those who defend them live in the subjunctive mood, where unreality reigns.

Those who were on to the *Dreams from My Father* composite character from the start weren't talking, and few across the country had interest in the junior U.S. Senator from Illinois. Collaborators in the media kept the truth from the public, but official biographer David Garrow, winner of the Pulitzer Prize, confirmed it in 2017:

Dreams from My Father was not a memoir or an autobiography; it was instead, in multitudinous ways, without any question *a work of historical fiction*. It featured many true-to-life figures and a bevy of accurately described events that indeed had occurred, but it employed the techniques and literary license of a novel, and its most important composite character was the narrator himself.

As Barry's girlfriend Genevieve Cook said, the composite character was a pompous jive who acts. Frank Marshall Davis' kinky exploits and Communist background made him politically radioactive. The Columbia students who never met him, and never knew anybody who did, thought that was strange, very strange. As the "ghetto raised" Columbia student said in *Barry*, this guy is "a whole different type of motherfucker."

After Gramps died, Barry and David Axelrod concocted the story about the Kenyan but as the reporter told Garrow, parts of it aren't true. In all his writings from 1958 to 1964, the Kenyan Barack Obama never mentioned an American wife and Hawaiian-born son.

Malik Obama, the Kenyan Barack Obama's son, now has it on the best authority that the American suddenly billed as his half-brother is indeed "a fraud and a con." But not just any fraud, and not just any con.

With a lot of help from his handlers, this fraud became president of the United States, the most powerful man in the world, for eight years. Evident from the start, the fakery has now been confirmed by the con's own biographer. At this writing, the media and critical establishments have yet to acknowledge the truth, and that is no surprise. To admit willful blindness is more than most can bear, but all is not lost.

Official, detailed acknowledgement of FDR's "splendid deception" took 40 years. After a similar span, the truth about President Franky Davis Jr. may gain widespread traction. In the meantime: and now abide fakes, hoaxes, and credulity, but the greatest of these is credulity.

Also by Lloyd Billingsley, available on Amazon.com

A Shut and Open Case

Double Murderer Mounts a Comeback in Davis, California

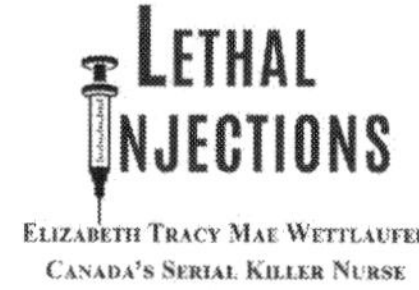

Lloyd Billingsley

Read all about it.

Made in the USA
Las Vegas, NV
04 May 2024

89420583R00081